Lizzie McGUIRE

© Disney

ALSO AVAILABLE FROM TOKYOPOP®

Lizzie McGuire

Volume 4

Series created by Terri Minsky

"I Do, I Don't"
written by Nina G. Bargiel & Jeremy J. Bargiel

"Come Fly With Me"
written by Douglas Tuber & Tim Maile

TOKYOPOP®

Los Angeles • Tokyo • London

Graphic Design & Lettering - Yolanda Petriz
Graphic Artists - Anna Kernbaum and Tomas Montalvo-Lagos
Cover Layout - Patrick Hook

Editor - Elizabeth Hurchalla
Managing Editor - Jill Freshney
Production Coordinator - Antonio DePietro
Production Manager - Jennifer Miller
Art Director - Matt Alford
Editorial Director - Jeremy Ross
VP of Production - Ron Klamert
President & C.O.O. - John Parker
Publisher & C.E.O. - Stuart Levy

Email: editor@TOKYOPOP.com
Come visit us online at www.TOKYOPOP.com

A **TOKYOPOP** Cine-Manga™
5900 Wilshire Blvd., Suite 2000, Los Angeles, CA 90036

Lizzie McGuire Volume 4

© 2003 Disney Enterprises, Inc.

ISBN: 1-59182-246-7

First TOKYOPOP printing: December 2003

10 9 8 7 6 5 4 3 2 1
Printed in Canada

Lizzie McGUiRE

Volume 4

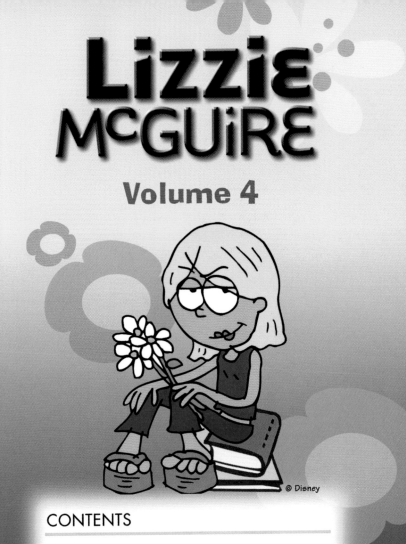

© Disney

CONTENTS

Lizzie McGuire

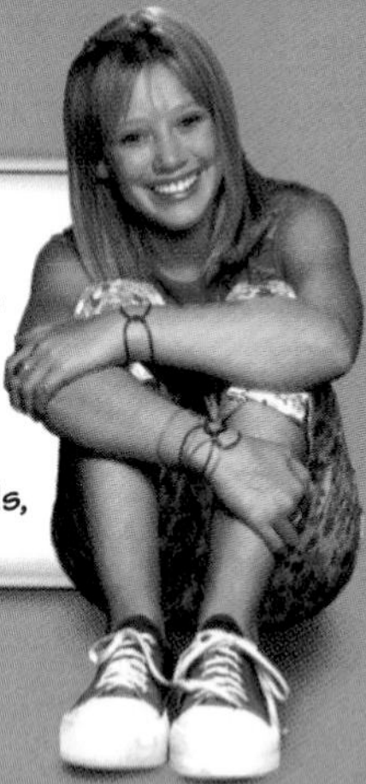

LIZZIE MCGUIRE:
A typical 14-year-old girl who has her fair share of bad hair days and embarrassing moments. Luckily, Lizzie knows how to admit when she's wrong, back up her friends, and stand up for herself.

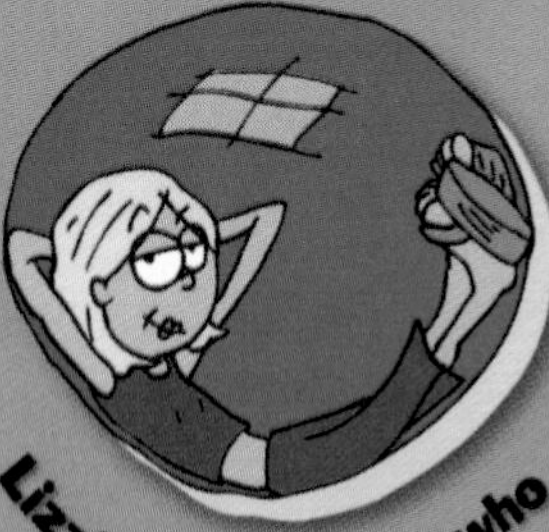

Lizzie's alter-ego, who says and does all the thing Lizzie's afraid to.

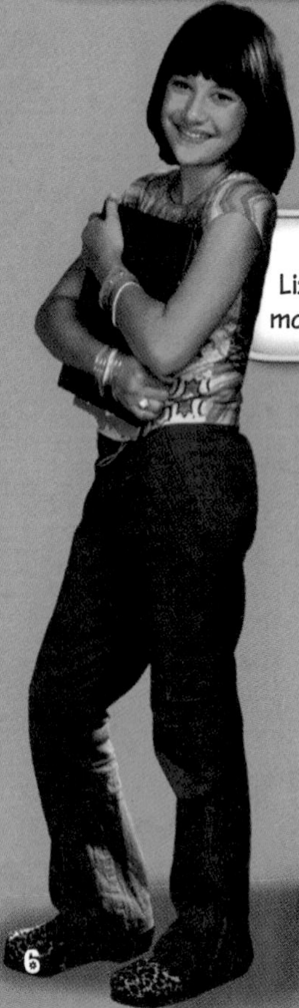

MIRANDA:
Lizzie's best friend and most trusted confidante.

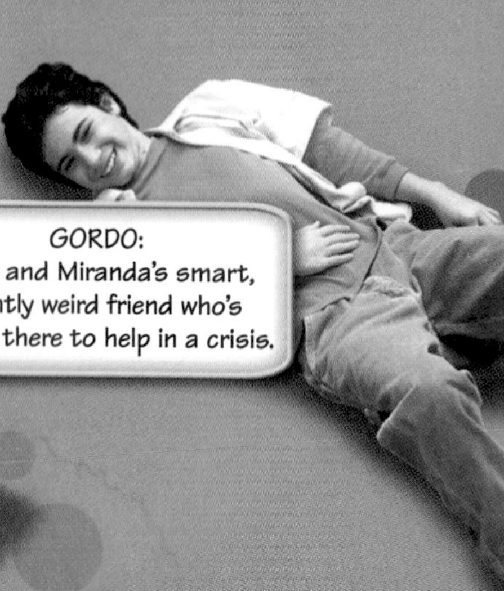

GORDO:
Lizzie and Miranda's smart, slightly weird friend who's always there to help in a crisis.

CHARACTER BIOS

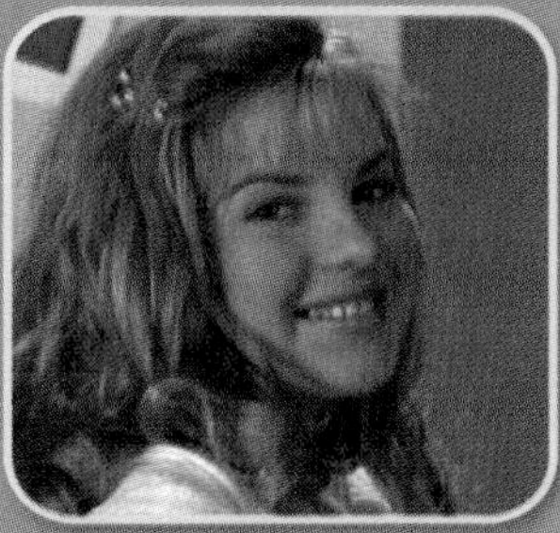

KATE:
Lizzie and Miranda's ex-friend who thinks she's too good for them now that she wears a bra.

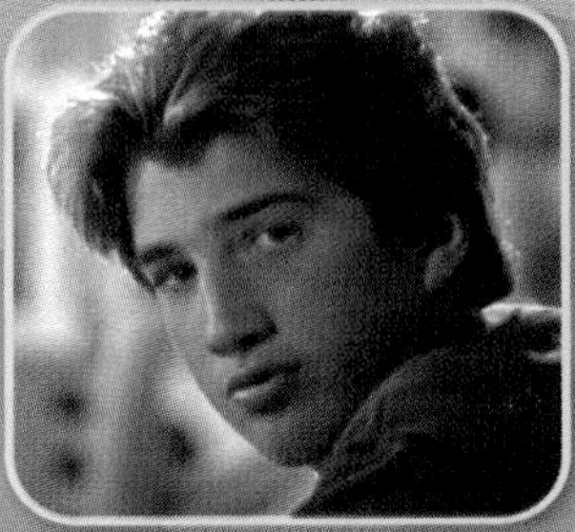

ETHAN:
The most popular guy in school.

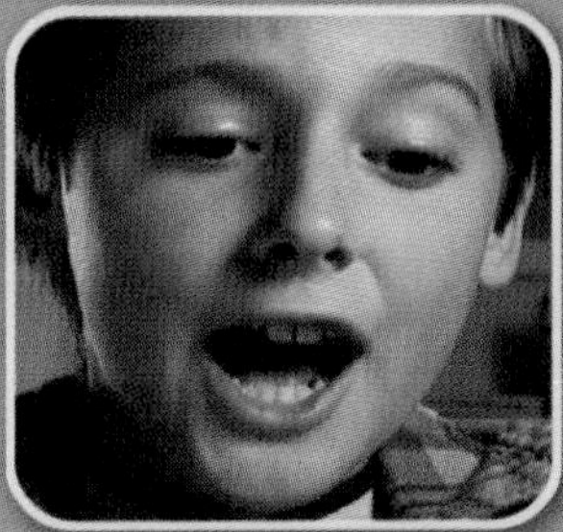

MATT:
Lizzie's little brother, who spends most of his time making her crazy.

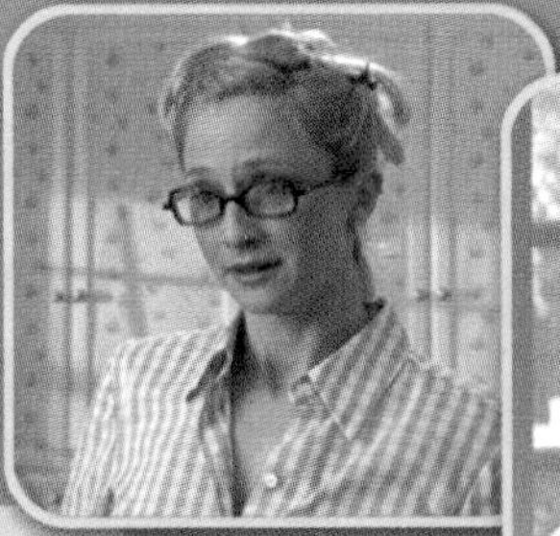

LIZZIE'S MOM, JO:
She only wants the best for Lizzie, but sometimes she tries a little too hard.

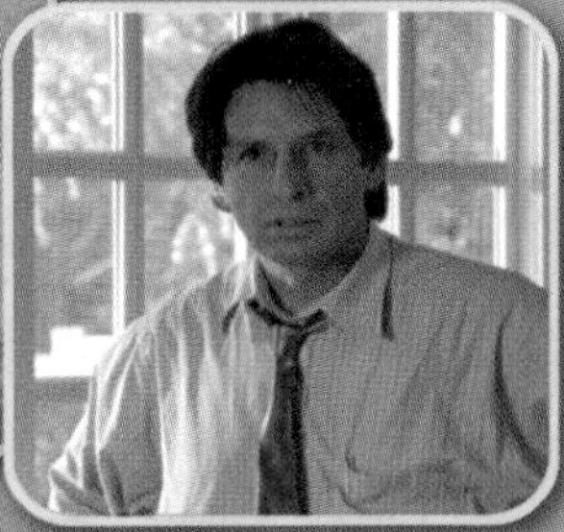

LIZZIE'S DAD, SAM:
He loves Lizzie, though he doesn't always know how to relate to her.

Lizzie McGuire

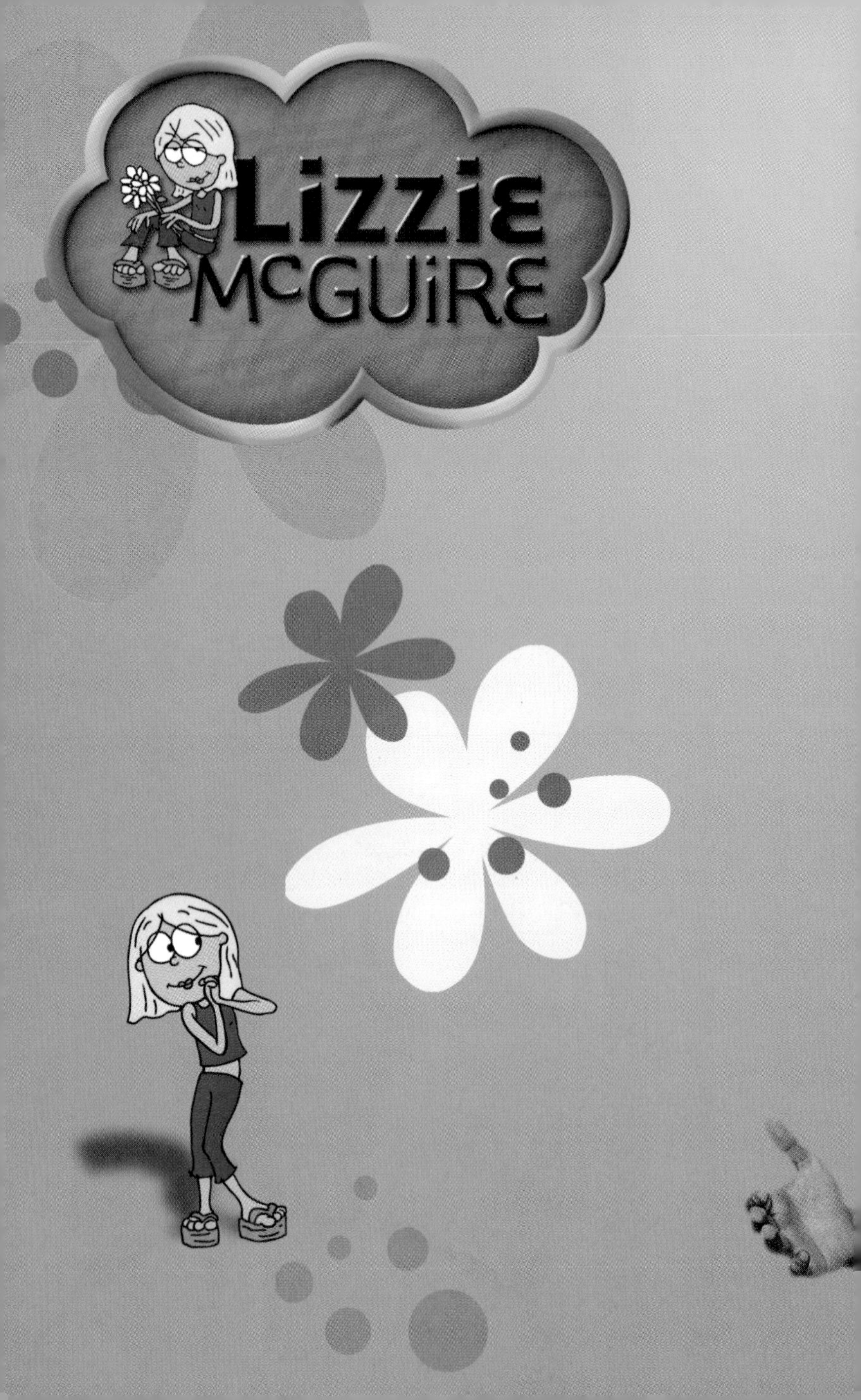

Episode 7

"I Do, I Don't"

Miranda is thrilled when she's paired with hearthrob Ethan for a social studies project. But when Lizzie discovers what's really behind Miranda's "mock marriage," she's forced to make a big decision. Should she tell Miranda the truth or protect a good friend's feelings?

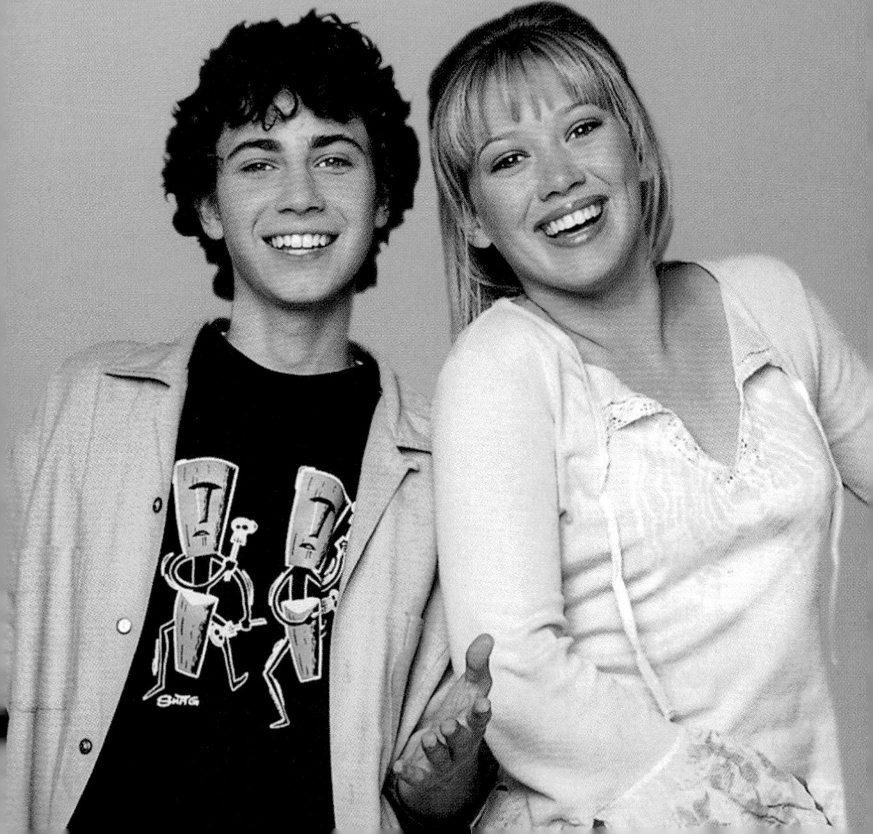

Face it, Miranda. It doesn't matter which X-Man you are.
You could be Mystique, that hot blue chick, and Ethan Craft wouldn't give you the time of day.
Which is why I'd be Rogue. I'd use my mutant power to suck away all of Kate's popularity. Ethan Craft would have no choice but to turn to me.
Or moi.
Great. Use the untapped powers of the universe to land a guy who's gonna end up working at a gas station. Part-time.
Hello? Ever heard of knocking?
Have you seen the flashlight?
No. On the phone. Leave.

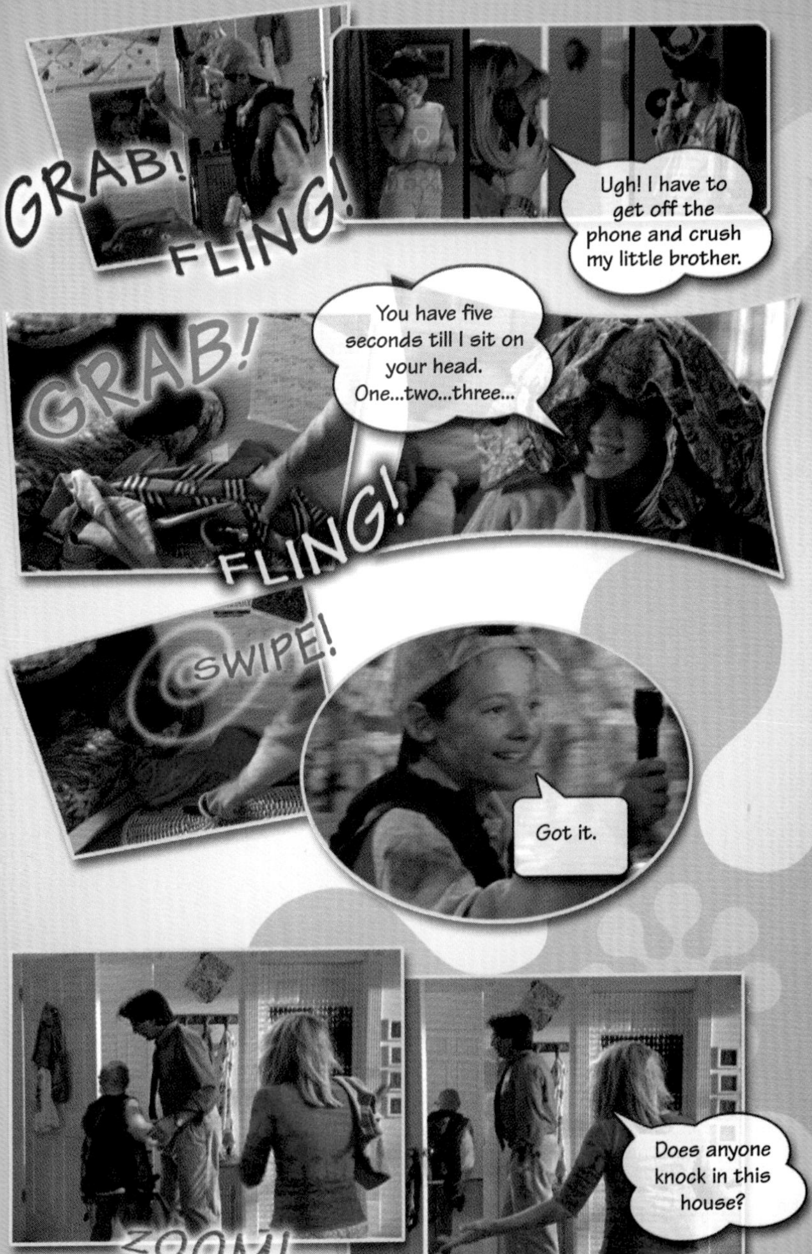
GRAB!
FLING!
Ugh! I have to get off the phone and crush my little brother.
GRAB!
You have five seconds till I sit on your head. One...two...three...
FLING!
SWIPE!
Got it.
ZOOM!
Does anyone knock in this house?

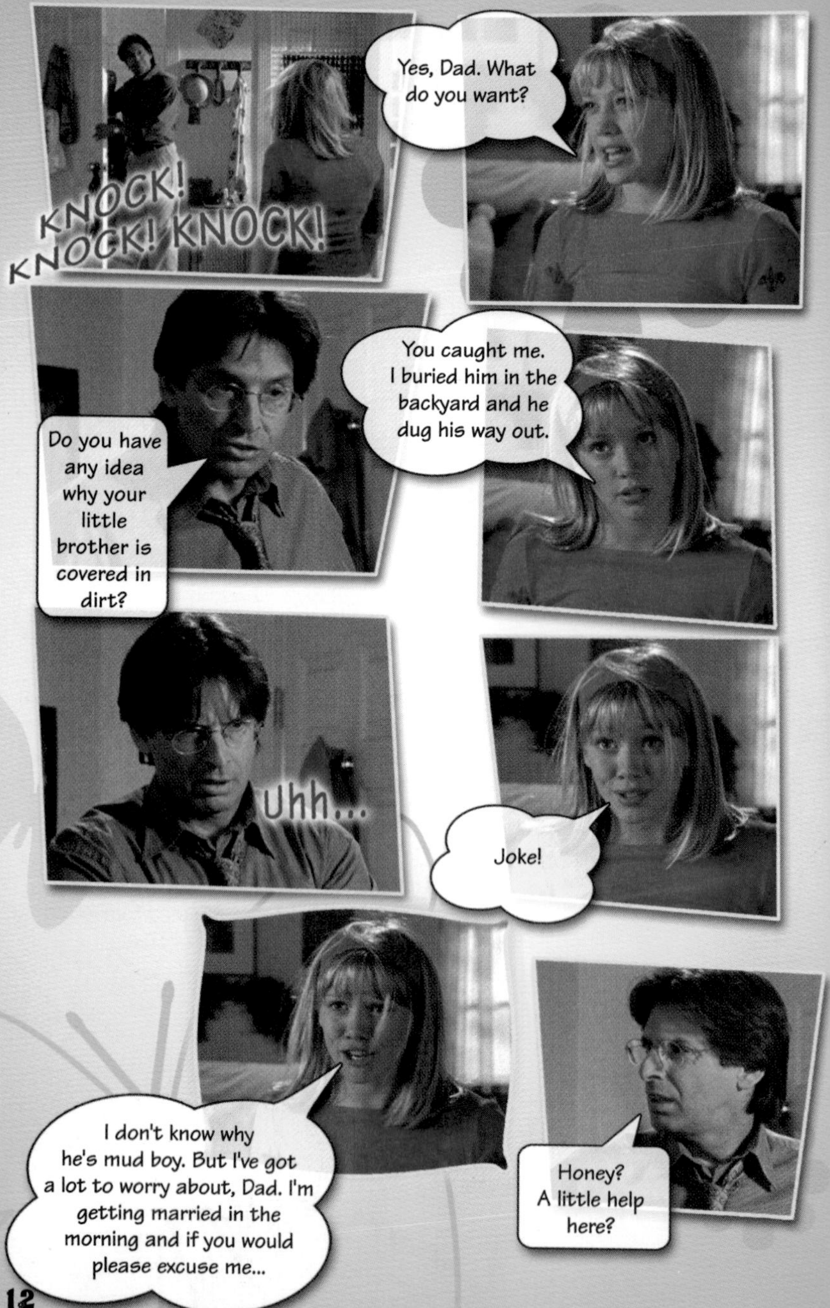

KNOCK! KNOCK! KNOCK!
Yes, Dad. What do you want?
Do you have any idea why your little brother is covered in dirt?
You caught me. I buried him in the backyard and he dug his way out.
Uhh...
Joke!
I don't know why he's mud boy. But I've got a lot to worry about, Dad. I'm getting married in the morning and if you would please excuse me...
Honey? A little help here?

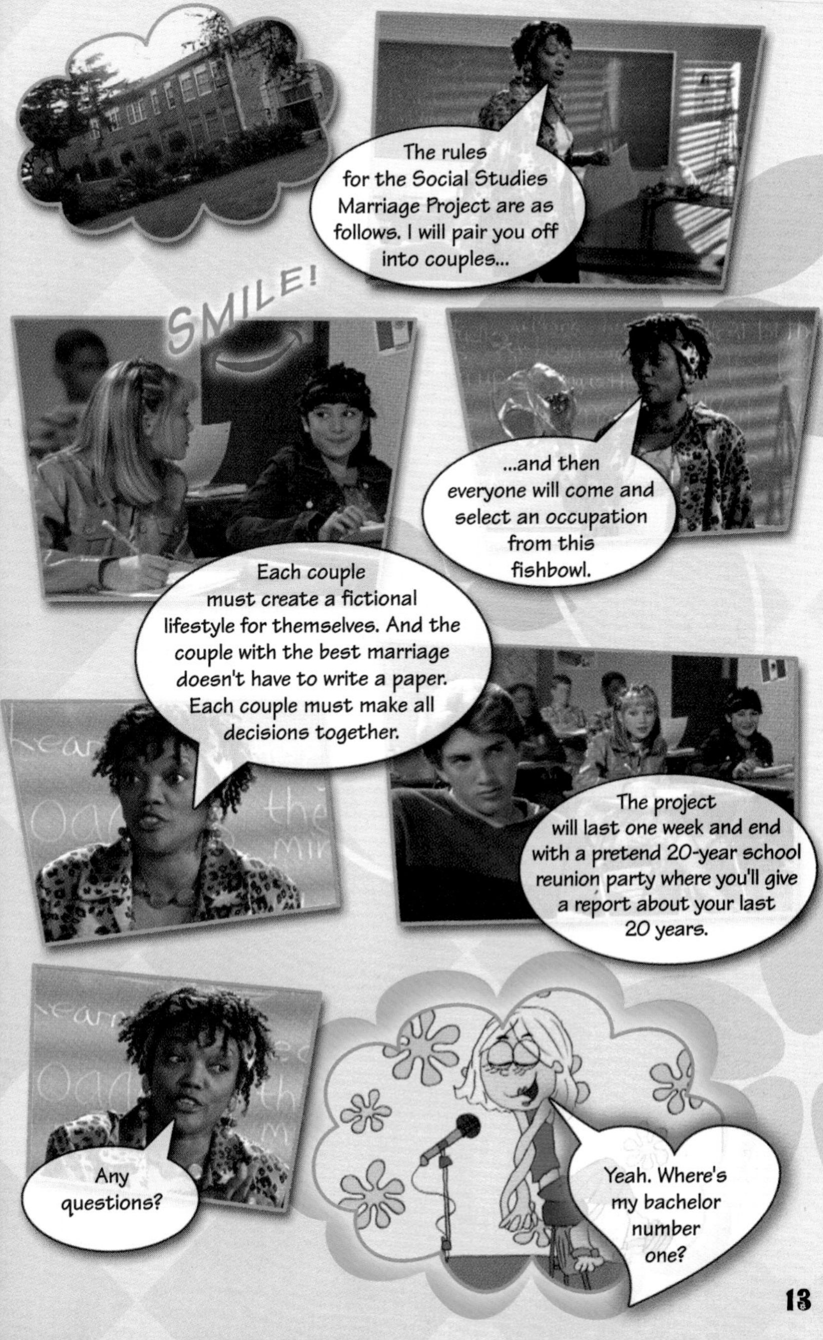
The rules for the Social Studies Marriage Project are as follows. I will pair you off into couples...
SMILE!
...and then everyone will come and select an occupation from this fishbowl.
Each couple must create a fictional lifestyle for themselves. And the couple with the best marriage doesn't have to write a paper. Each couple must make all decisions together.
The project will last one week and end with a pretend 20-year school reunion party where you'll give a report about your last 20 years.
Any questions?
Yeah. Where's my bachelor number one?

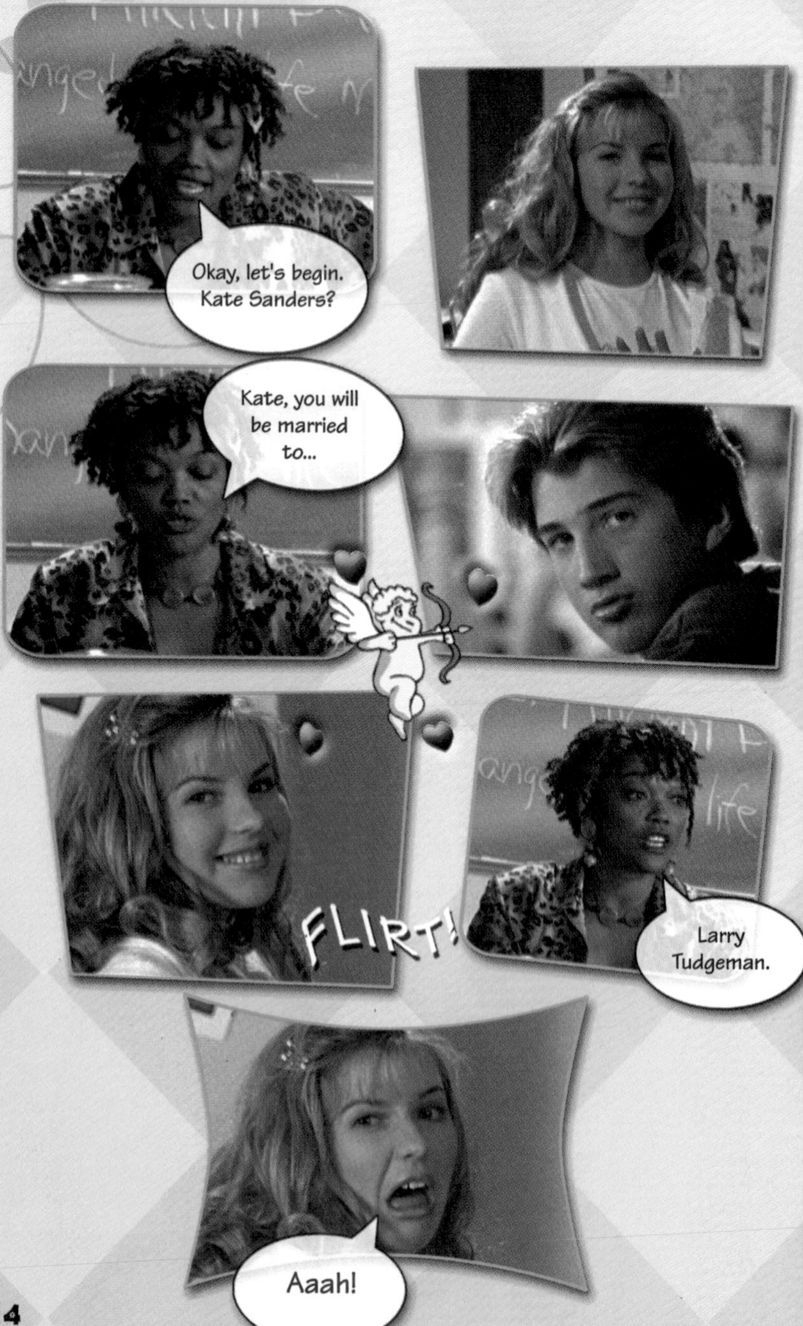

Okay, let's begin. Kate Sanders?
Kate, you will be married to...
FLIRT!
Larry Tudgeman.
Aaah!

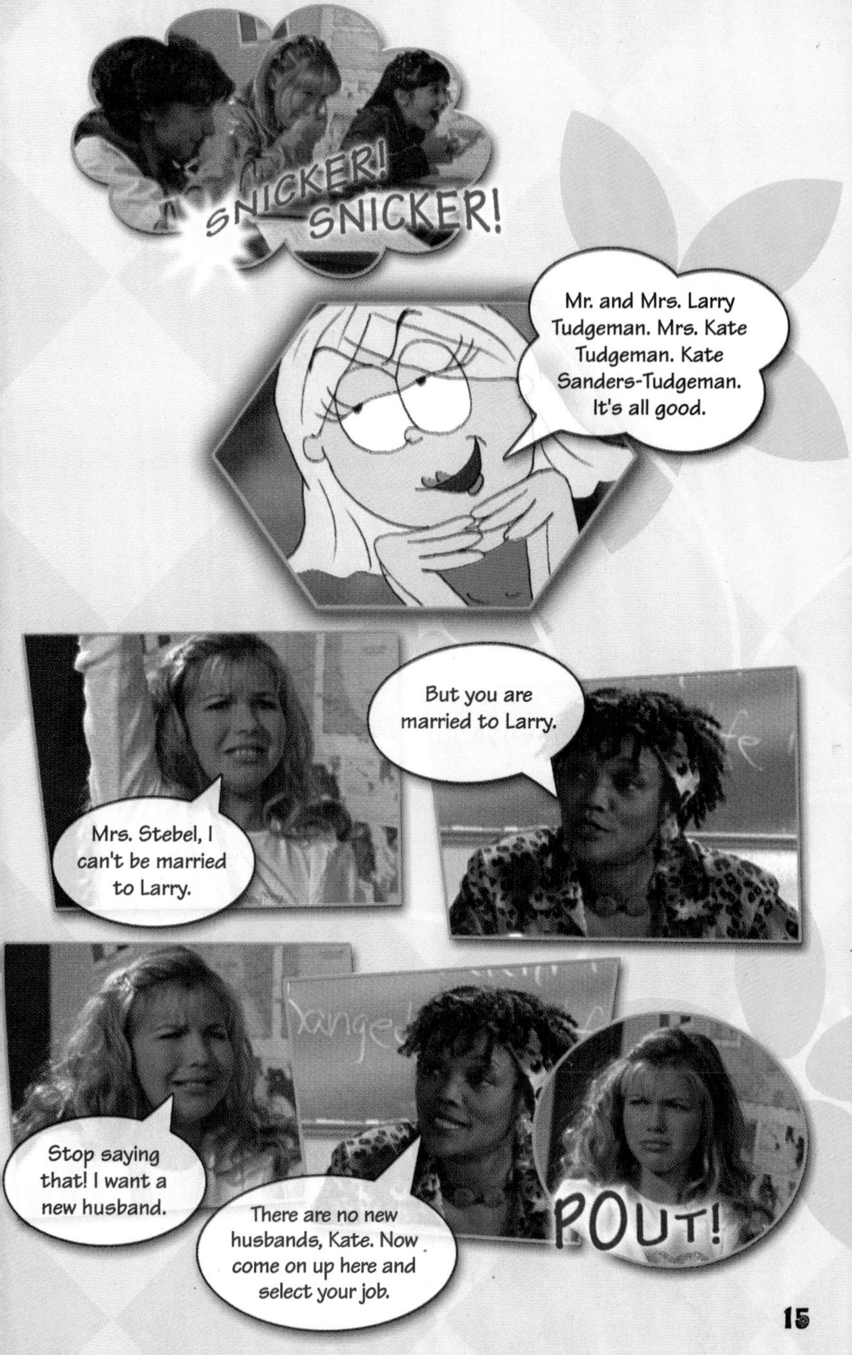
SNICKER! SNICKER!
Mr. and Mrs. Larry Tudgeman. Mrs. Kate Tudgeman. Kate Sanders-Tudgeman. It's all good.
Mrs. Stebel, I can't be married to Larry.
But you are married to Larry.
Stop saying that! I want a new husband.
There are no new husbands, Kate. Now come on up here and select your job.
POUT!

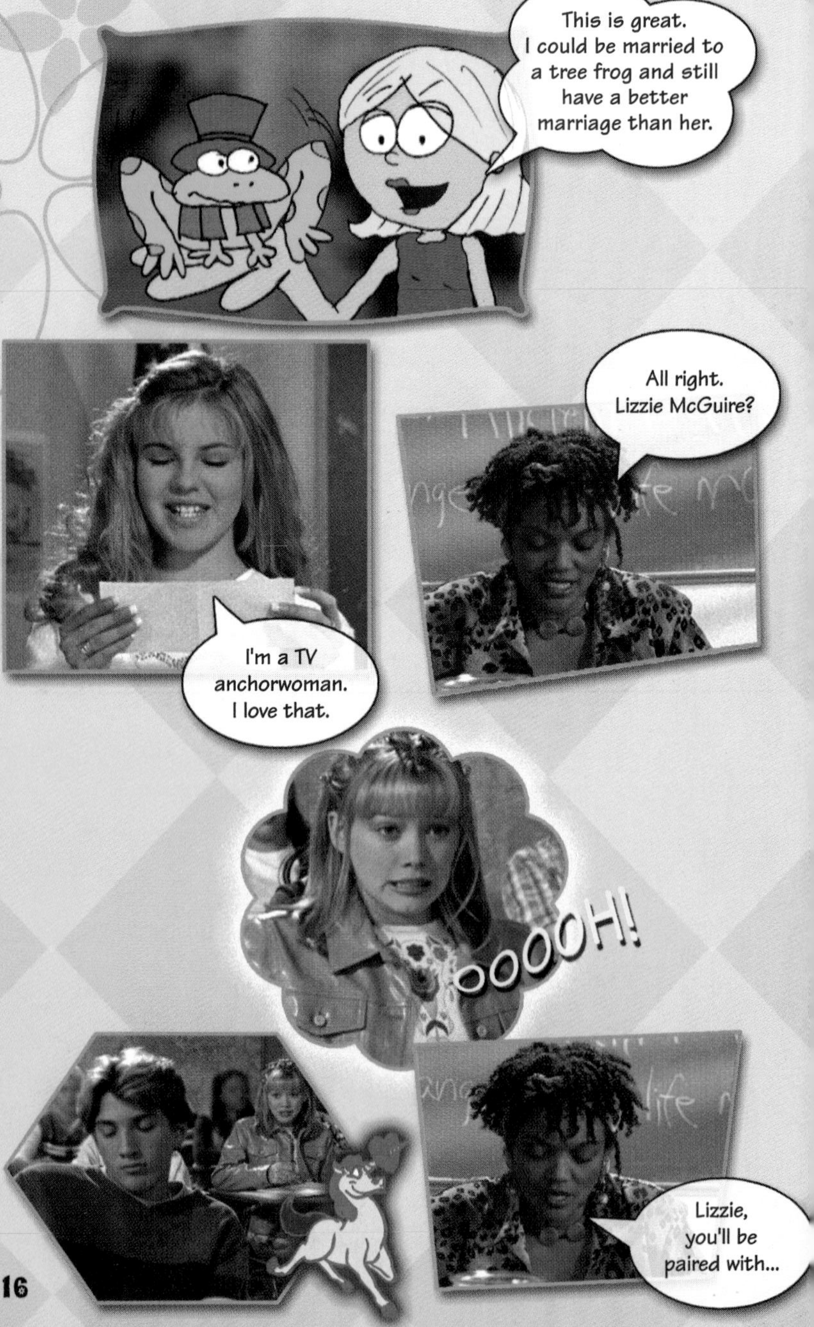
This is great. I could be married to a tree frog and still have a better marriage than her.
I'm a TV anchorwoman. I love that.
All right. Lizzie McGuire?
OOOOH!
Lizzie, you'll be paired with...

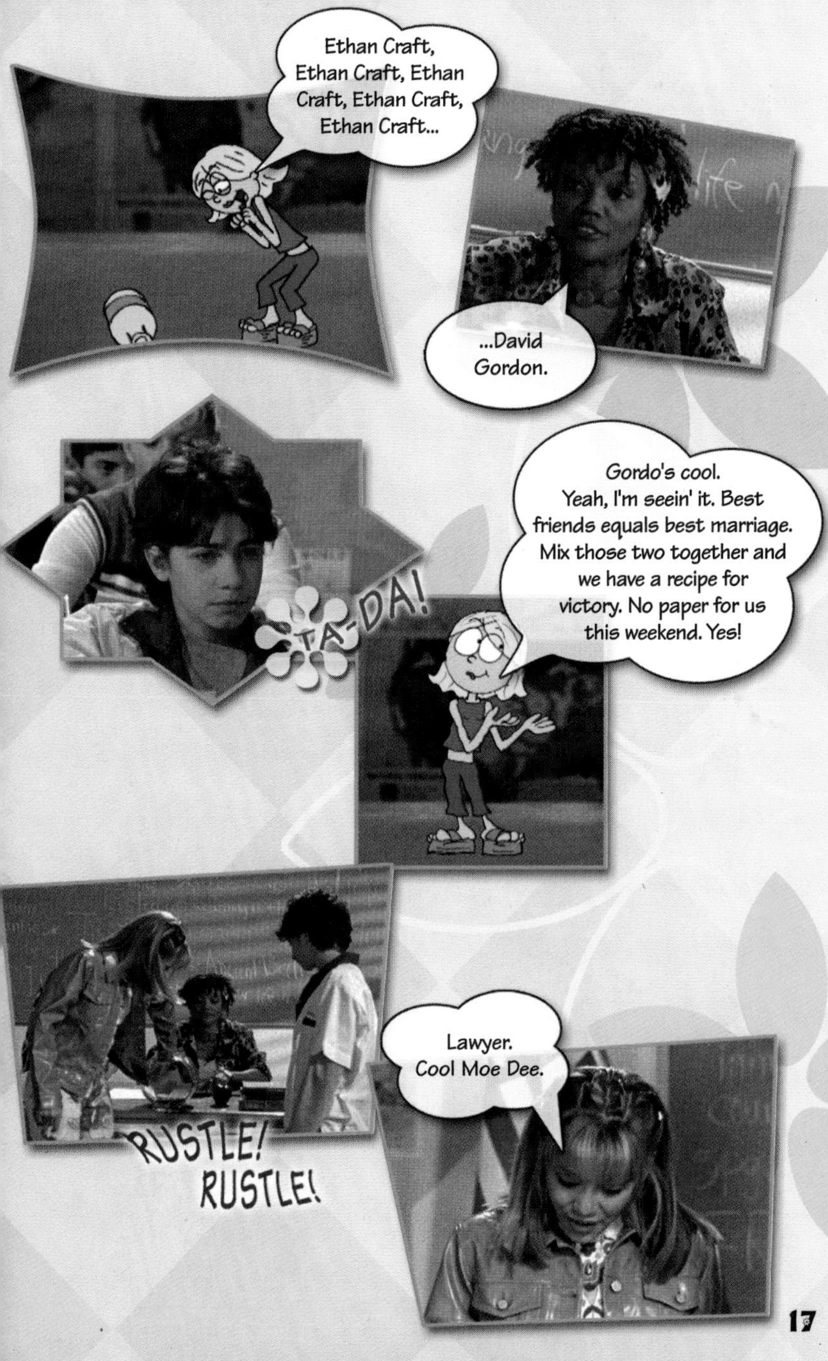
Ethan Craft, Ethan Craft, Ethan Craft, Ethan Craft, Ethan Craft...
...David Gordon.
TA-DA!
Gordo's cool. Yeah, I'm seein' it. Best friends equals best marriage. Mix those two together and we have a recipe for victory. No paper for us this weekend. Yes!
RUSTLE! RUSTLE!
Lawyer. Cool Moe Dee.

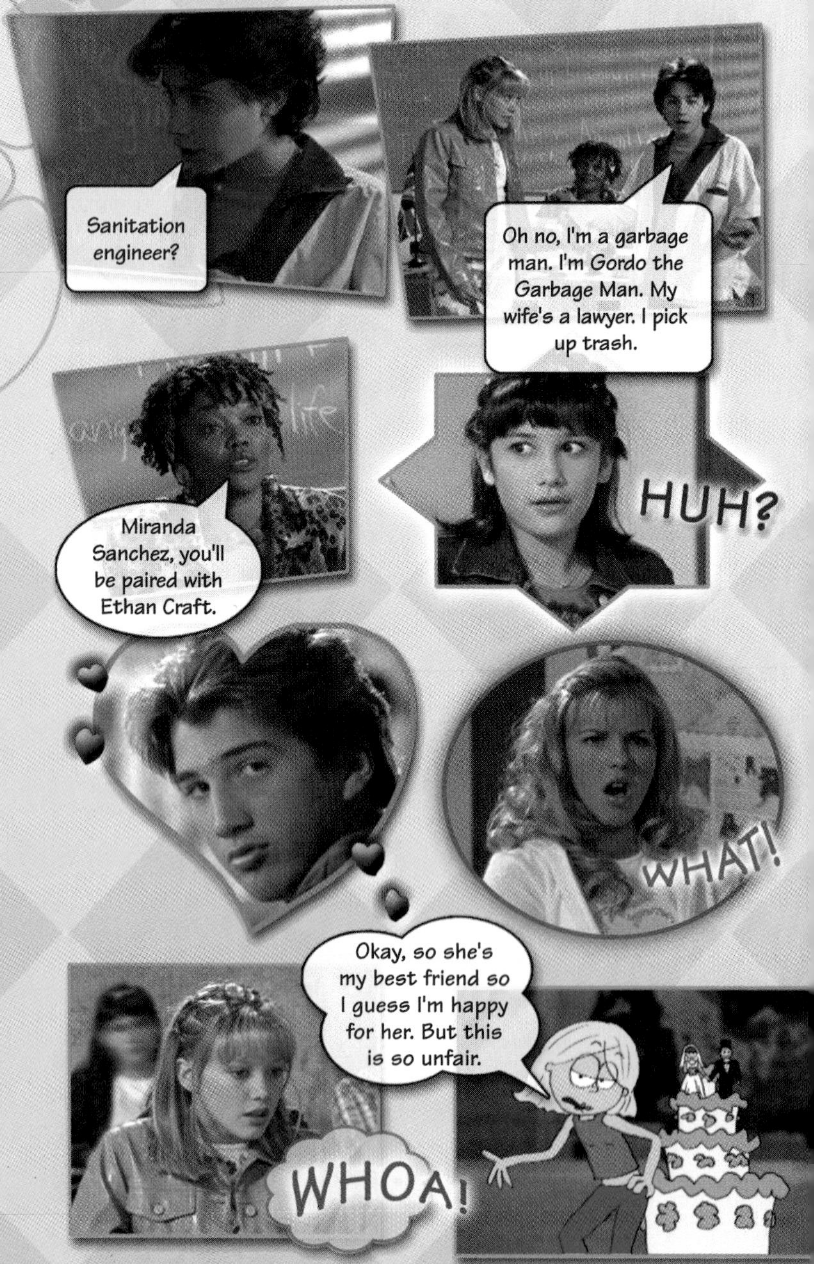
Sanitation engineer?
Oh no, I'm a garbage man. I'm Gordo the Garbage Man. My wife's a lawyer. I pick up trash.
Miranda Sanchez, you'll be paired with Ethan Craft.
HUH?
WHAT!
Okay, so she's my best friend so I guess I'm happy for her. But this is so unfair.
WHOA!

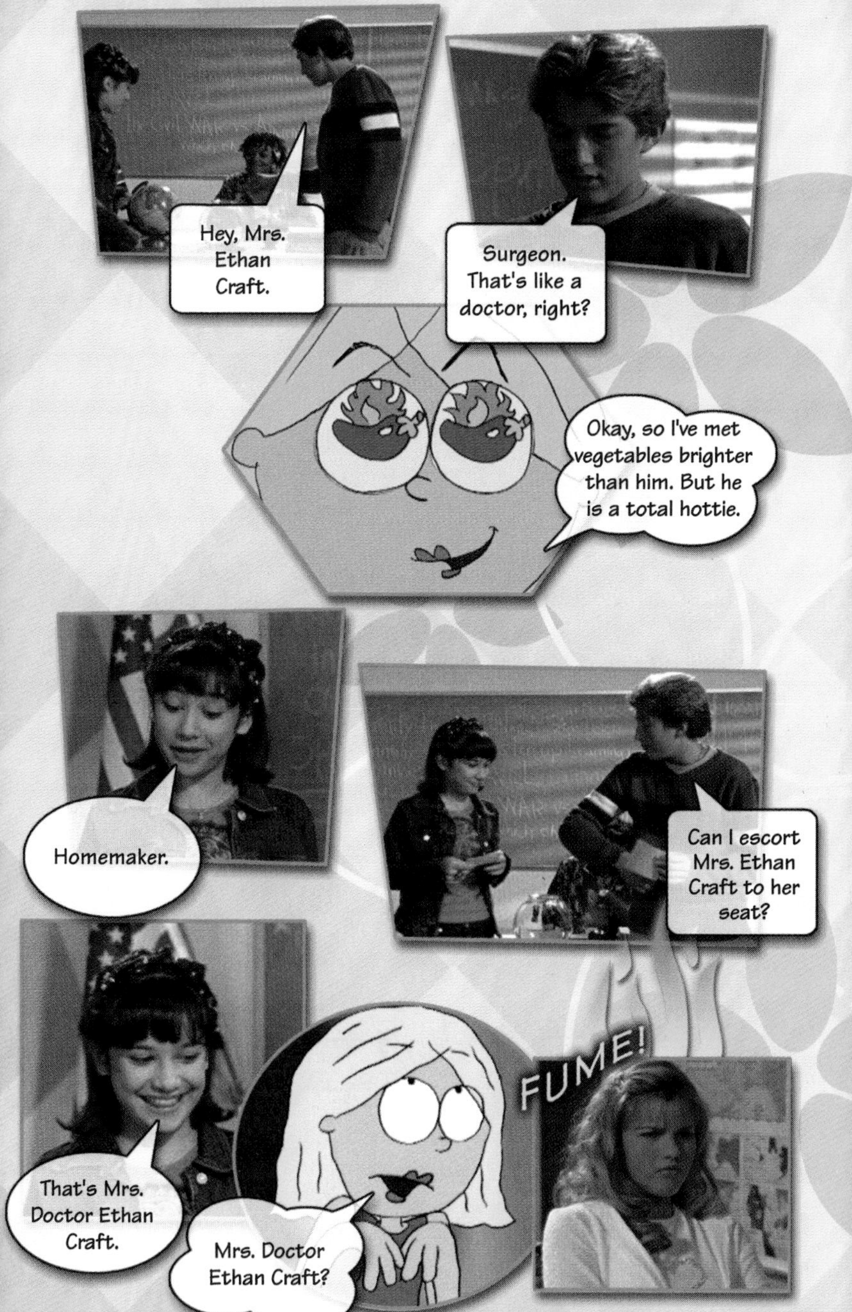

Hey, Mrs. Ethan Craft.
Surgeon. That's like a doctor, right?
Okay, so I've met vegetables brighter than him. But he is a total hottie.
Homemaker.
Can I escort Mrs. Ethan Craft to her seat?
That's Mrs. Doctor Ethan Craft.
Mrs. Doctor Ethan Craft?
FUME!

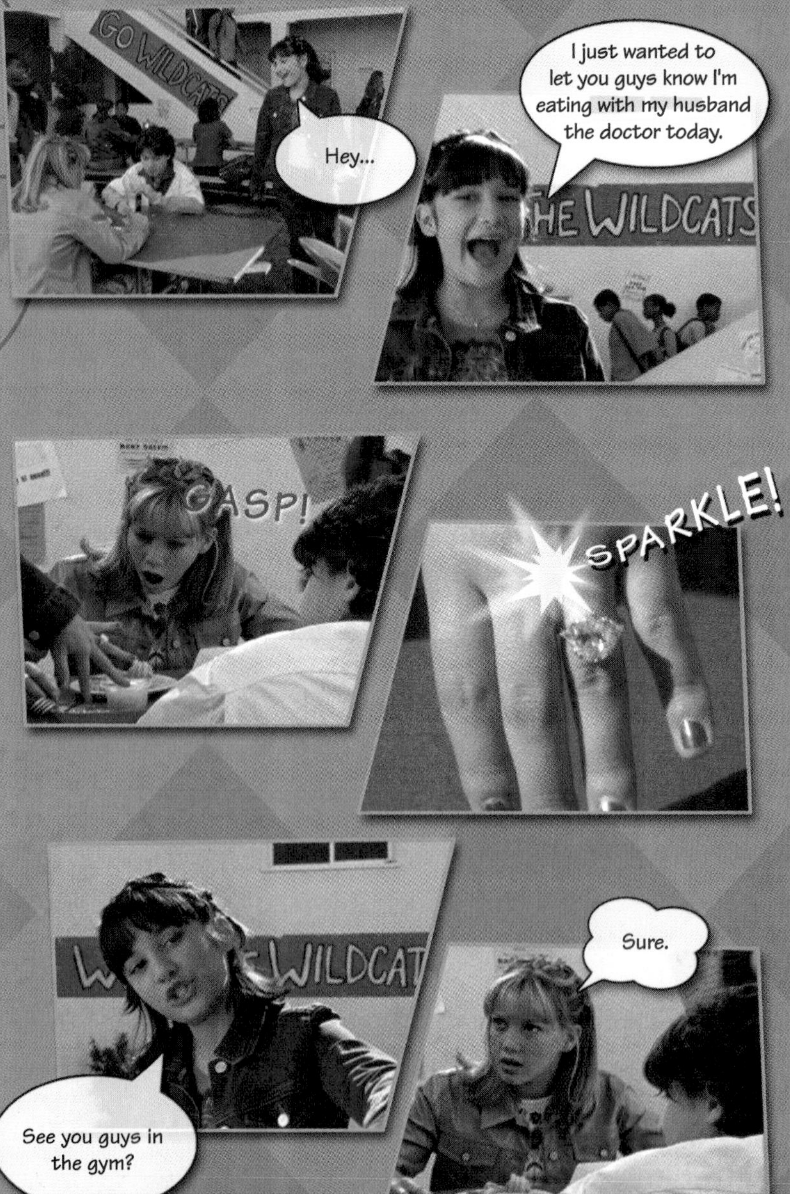
GO WILDCATS
Hey...
I just wanted to let you guys know I'm eating with my husband the doctor today.
HE WILDCATS
GASP!
SPARKLE!
WILDCAT
See you guys in the gym?
Sure.

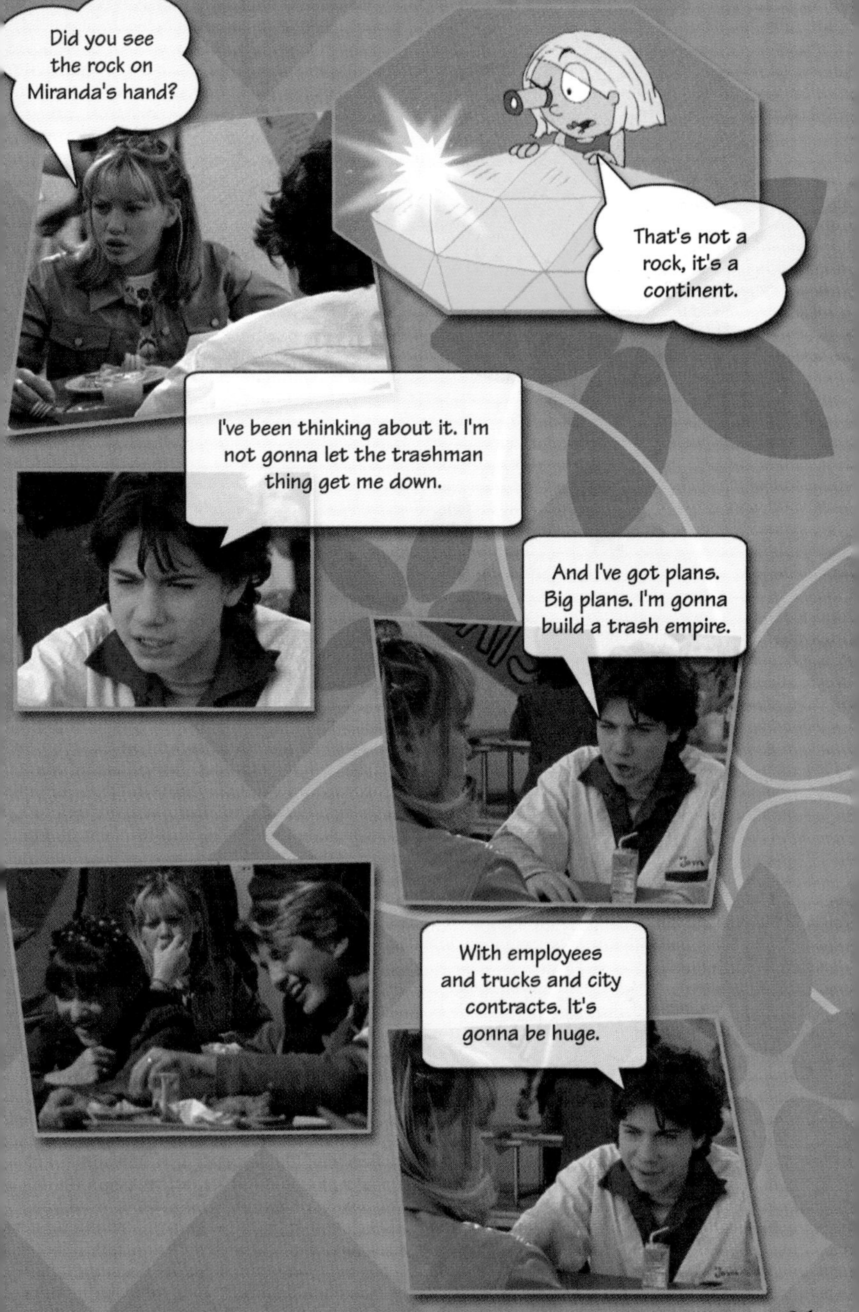

Did you see the rock on Miranda's hand?
That's not a rock, it's a continent.
I've been thinking about it. I'm not gonna let the trashman thing get me down.
And I've got plans. Big plans. I'm gonna build a trash empire.
With employees and trucks and city contracts. It's gonna be huge.

The key is one truck. Just one garbage truck.

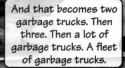

And that becomes two garbage trucks. Then three. Then a lot of garbage trucks. A fleet of garbage trucks.

For you see, trucks equal contracts and contracts equal money and money equals power.

Are you even listening to me?

MMM?

SNAP!

Hello!

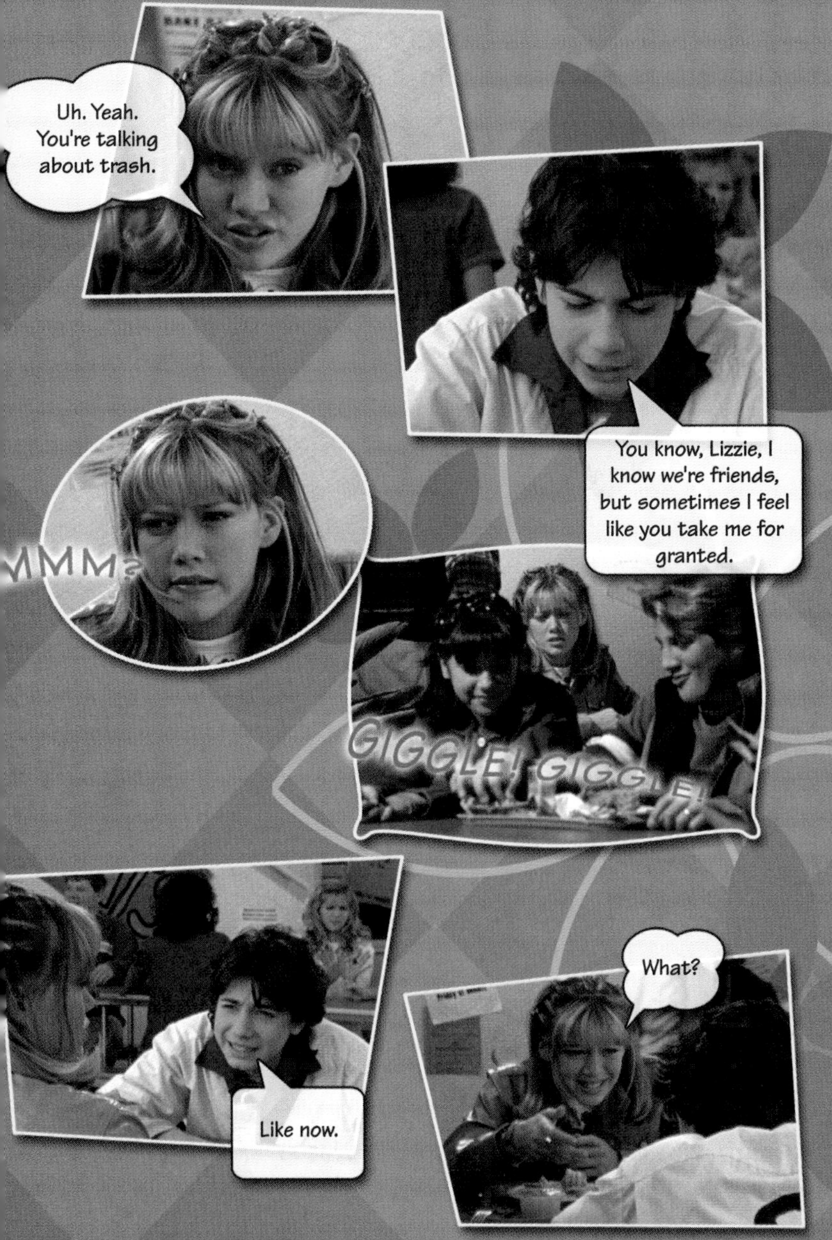
Uh. Yeah. You're talking about trash.
You know, Lizzie, I know we're friends, but sometimes I feel like you take me for granted.
GIGGLE! GIGGLE!
Like now.
What?

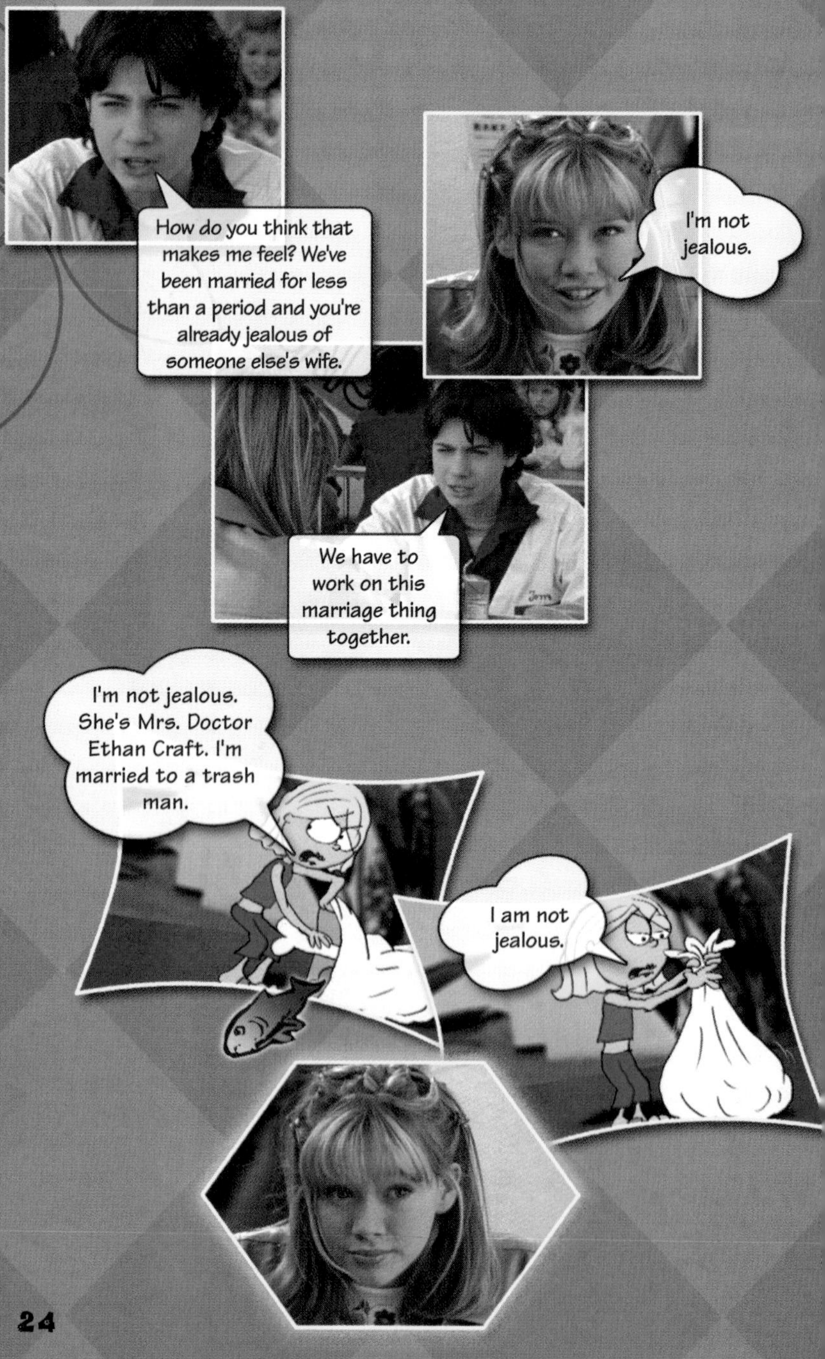
How do you think that makes me feel? We've been married for less than a period and you're already jealous of someone else's wife.
I'm not jealous.
We have to work on this marriage thing together.
I'm not jealous. She's Mrs. Doctor Ethan Craft. I'm married to a trash man.
I am not jealous.

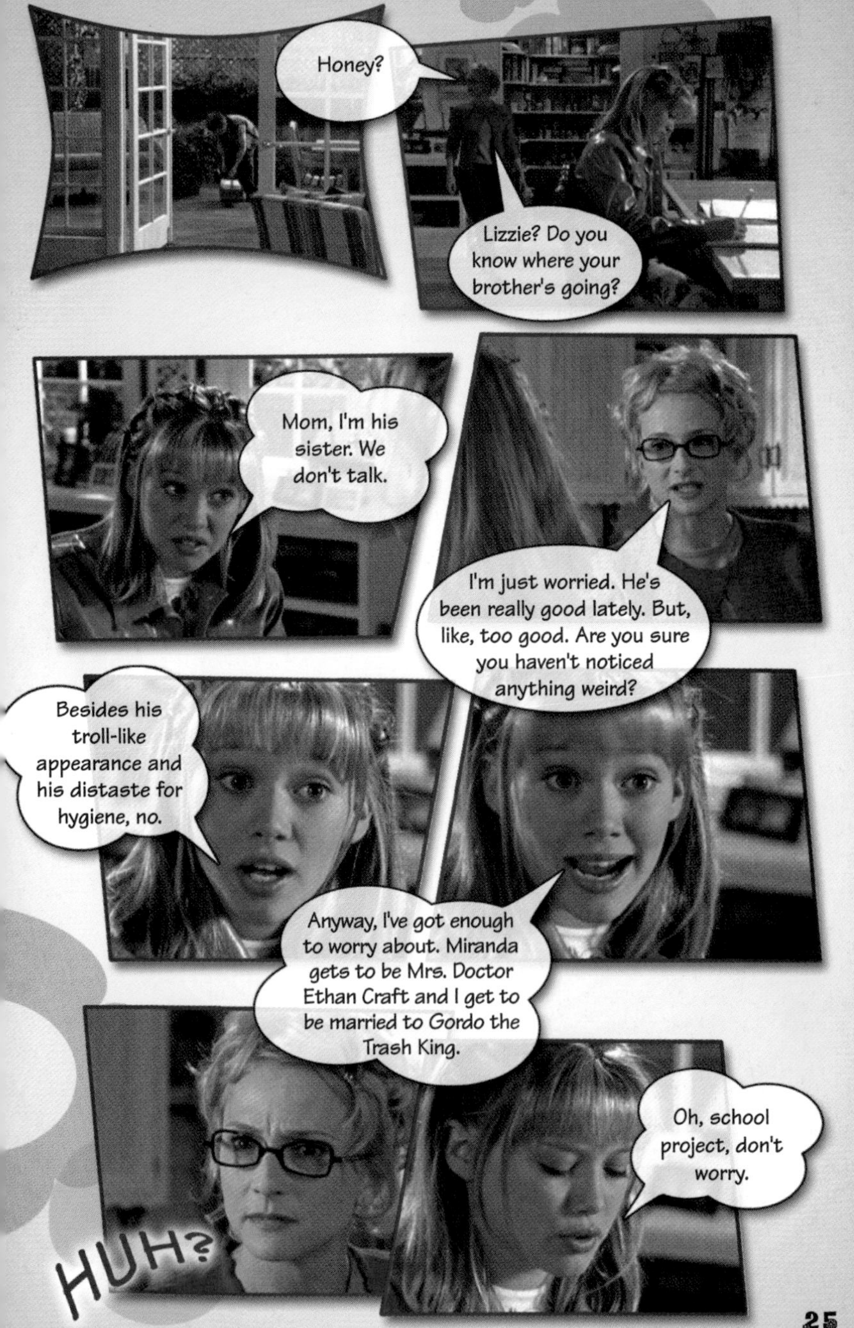
Honey?
Lizzie? Do you know where your brother's going?
Mom, I'm his sister. We don't talk.
I'm just worried. He's been really good lately. But, like, too good. Are you sure you haven't noticed anything weird?
Besides his troll-like appearance and his distaste for hygiene, no.
Anyway, I've got enough to worry about. Miranda gets to be Mrs. Doctor Ethan Craft and I get to be married to Gordo the Trash King.
HUH?
Oh, school project, don't worry.

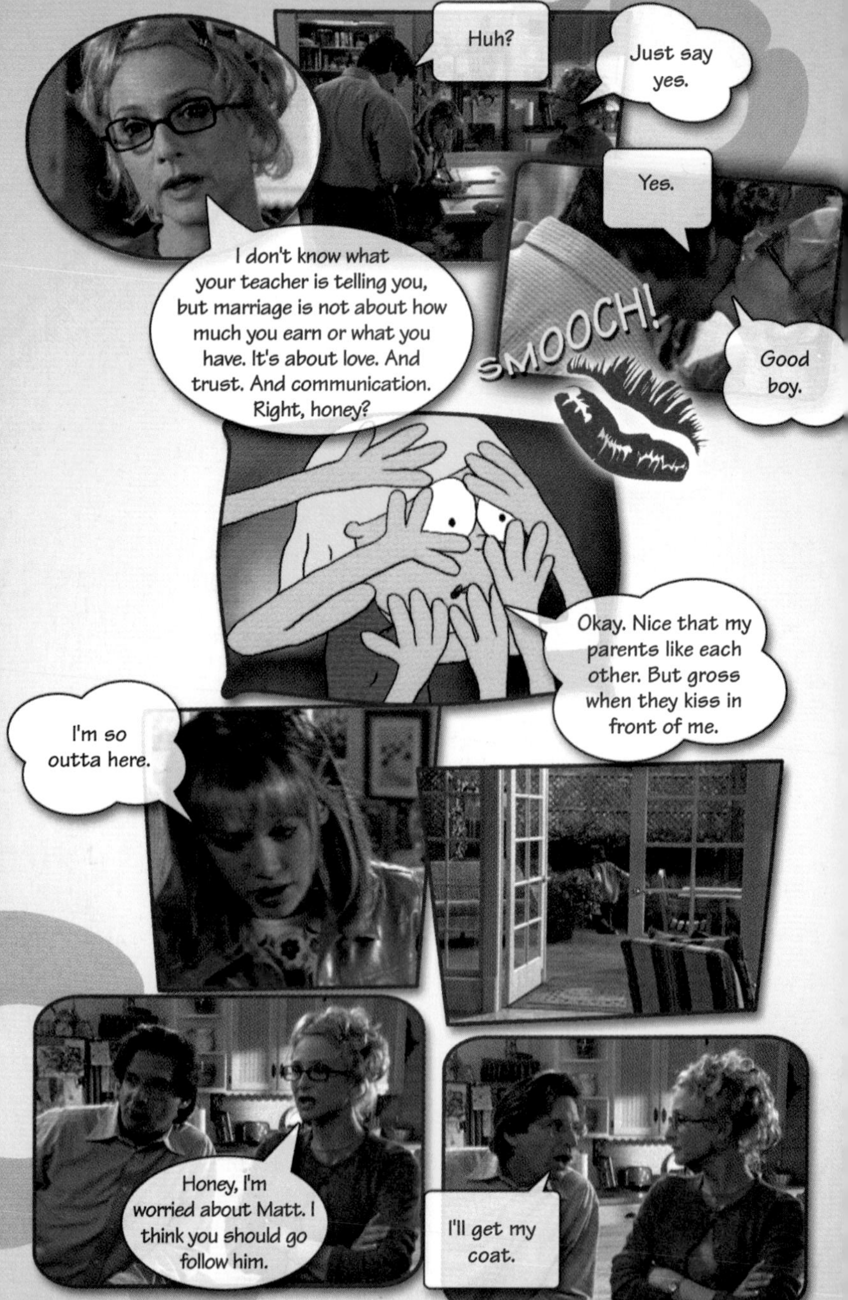
Huh?
Just say yes.
Yes.
I don't know what your teacher is telling you, but marriage is not about how much you earn or what you have. It's about love. And trust. And communication. Right, honey?
SMOOCH!
Good boy.
Okay. Nice that my parents like each other. But gross when they kiss in front of me.
I'm so outta here.
Honey, I'm worried about Matt. I think you should go follow him.
I'll get my coat.

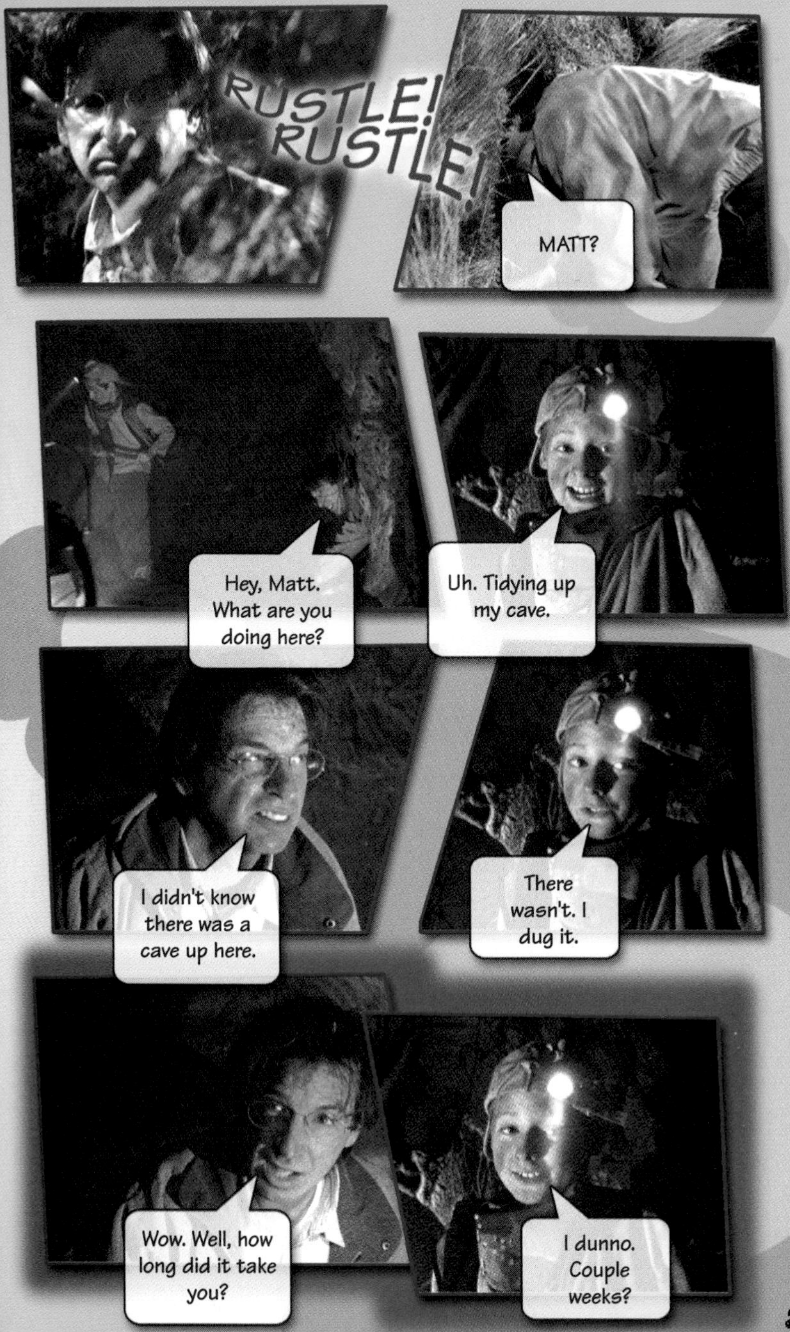
RUSTLE! RUSTLE!
MATT?
Hey, Matt. What are you doing here?
Uh. Tidying up my cave.
I didn't know there was a cave up here.
There wasn't. I dug it.
Wow. Well, how long did it take you?
I dunno. Couple weeks?

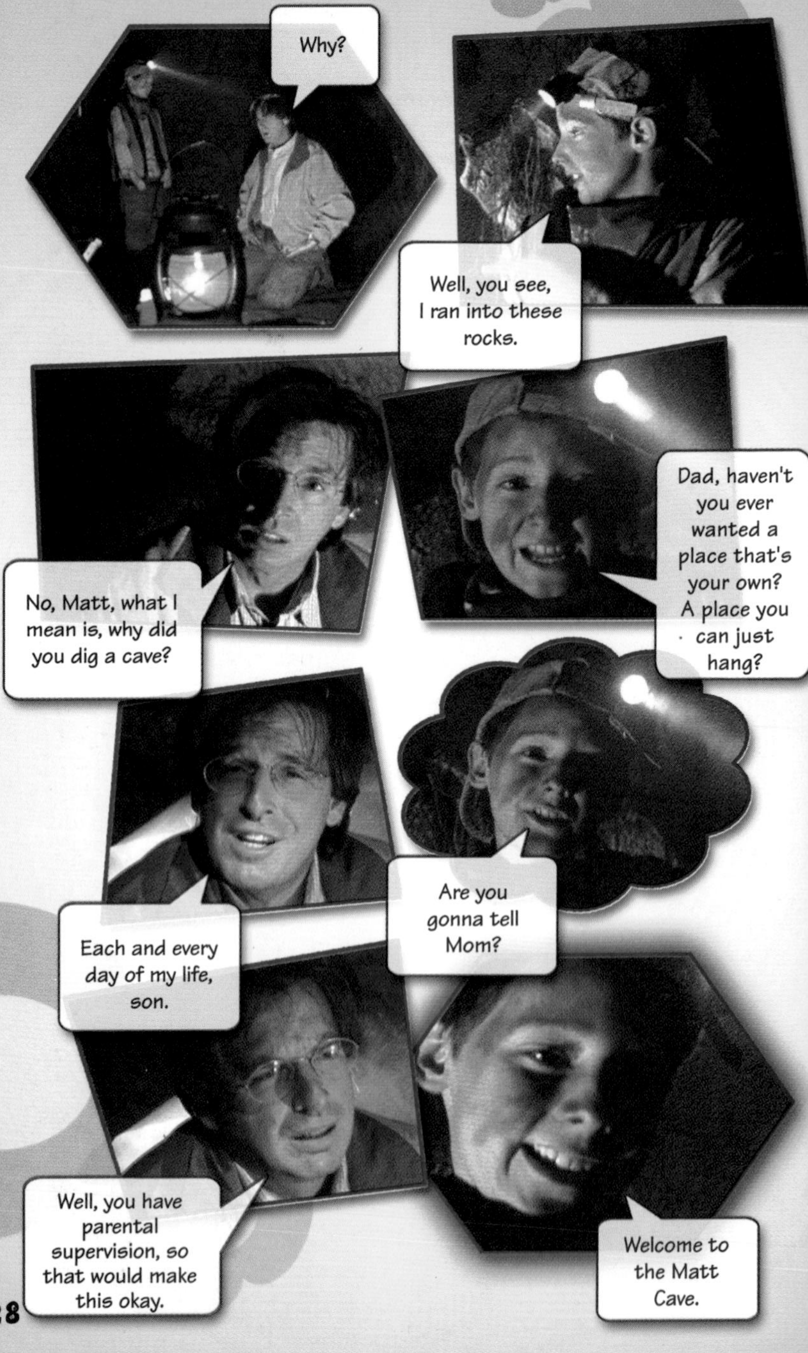
Why?
Well, you see, I ran into these rocks.
No, Matt, what I mean is, why did you dig a cave?
Dad, haven't you ever wanted a place that's your own? A place you can just hang?
Each and every day of my life, son.
Are you gonna tell Mom?
Well, you have parental supervision, so that would make this okay.
Welcome to the Matt Cave.

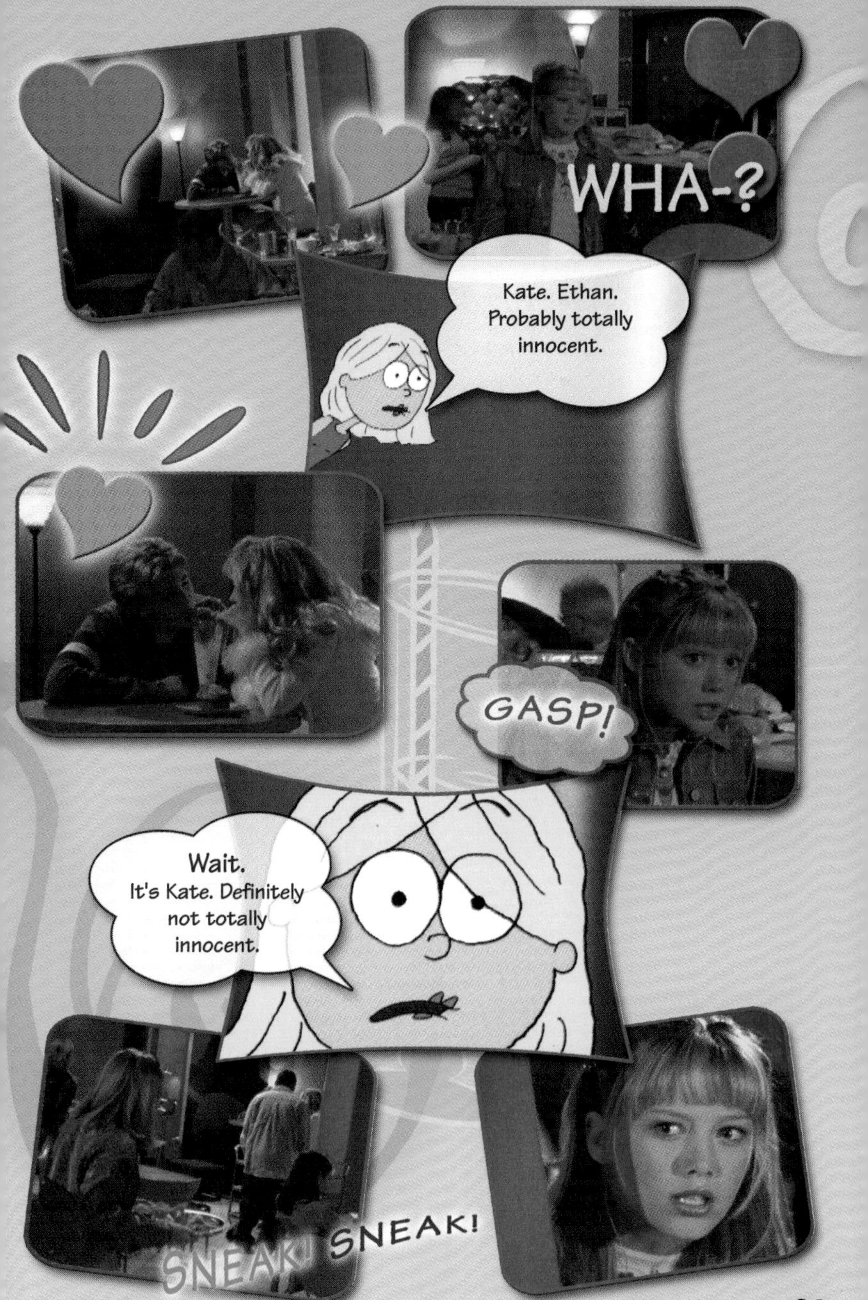

WHA-?
Kate. Ethan. Probably totally innocent.
GASP!
Wait. It's Kate. Definitely not totally innocent.
SNEAK! SNEAK!

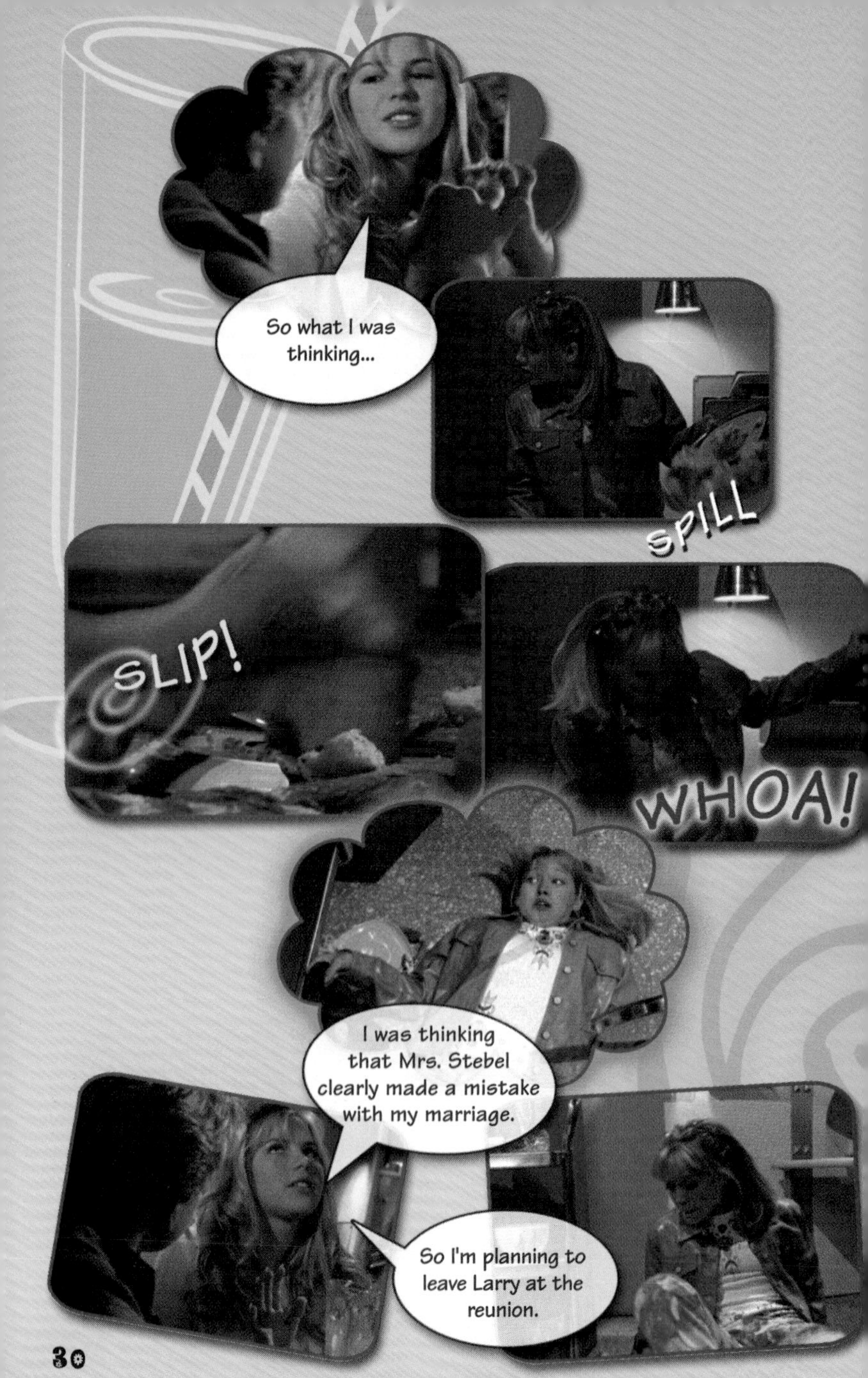
So what I was thinking...
SPILL
SLIP!
WHOA!
I was thinking that Mrs. Stebel clearly made a mistake with my marriage.
So I'm planning to leave Larry at the reunion.

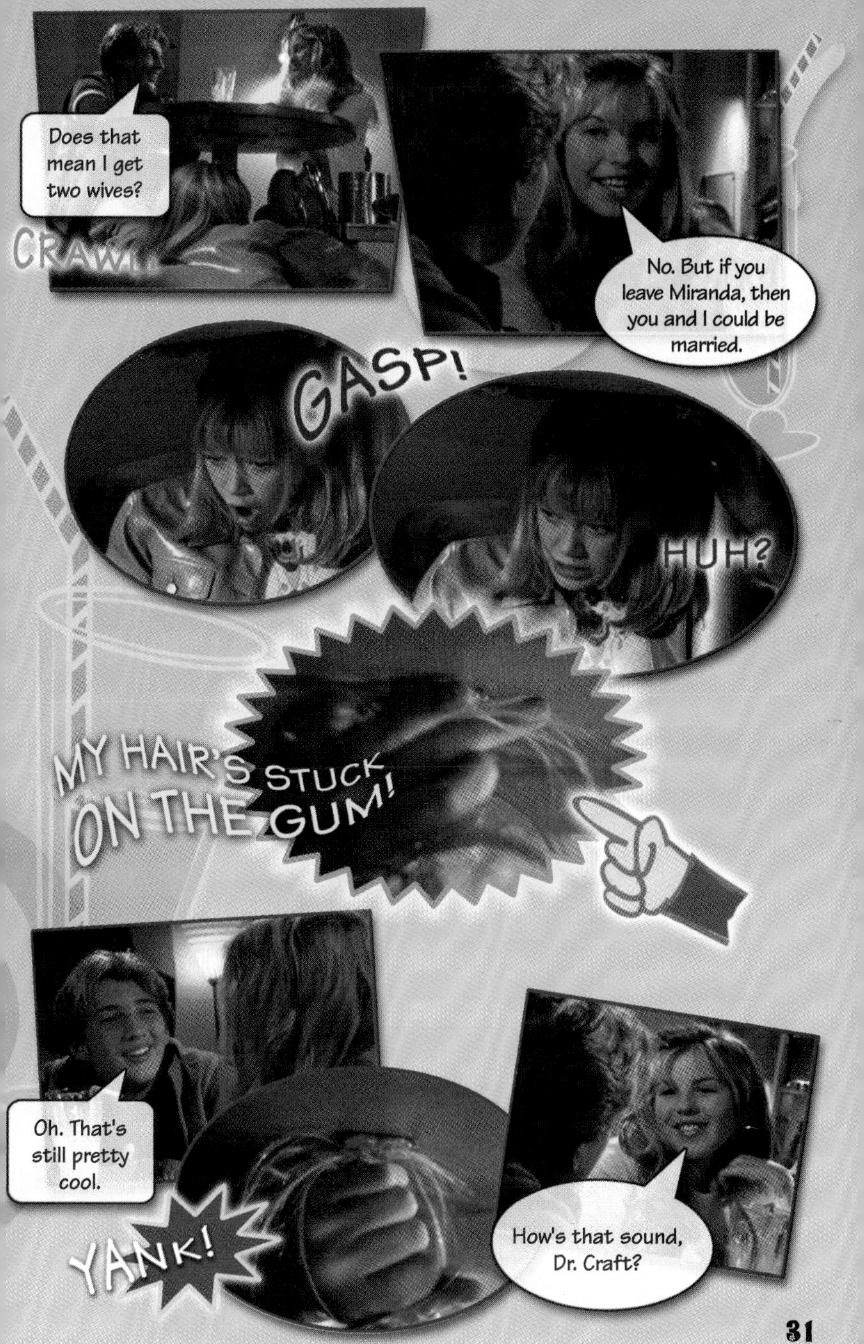
Does that mean I get two wives?
CRAWL
No. But if you leave Miranda, then you and I could be married.
GASP!
HUH?
MY HAIR'S STUCK ON THE GUM!
Oh. That's still pretty cool.
YANK!
How's that sound, Dr. Craft?

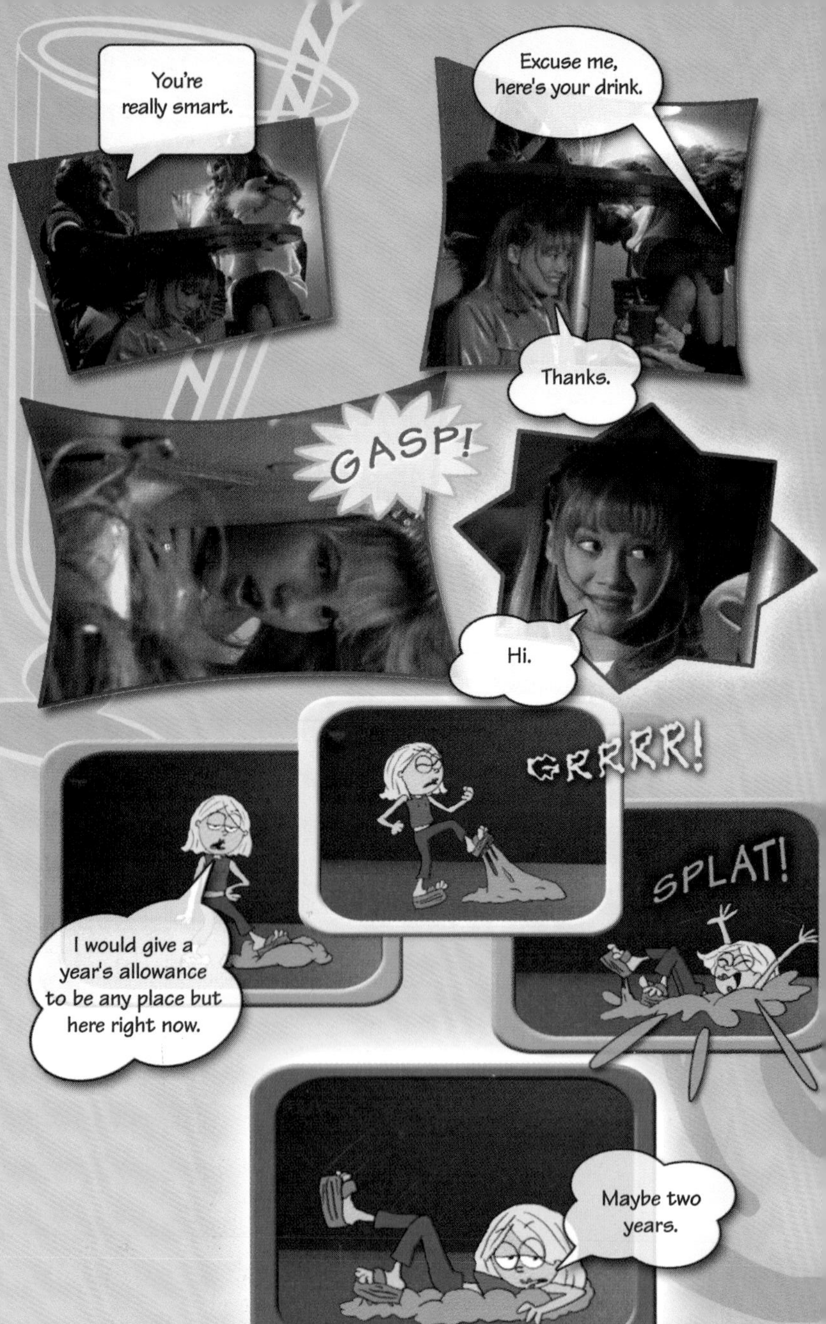

You're really smart.
Excuse me, here's your drink.
Thanks.
GASP!
Hi.
GRRRR!
I would give a year's allowance to be any place but here right now.
SPLAT!
Maybe two years.

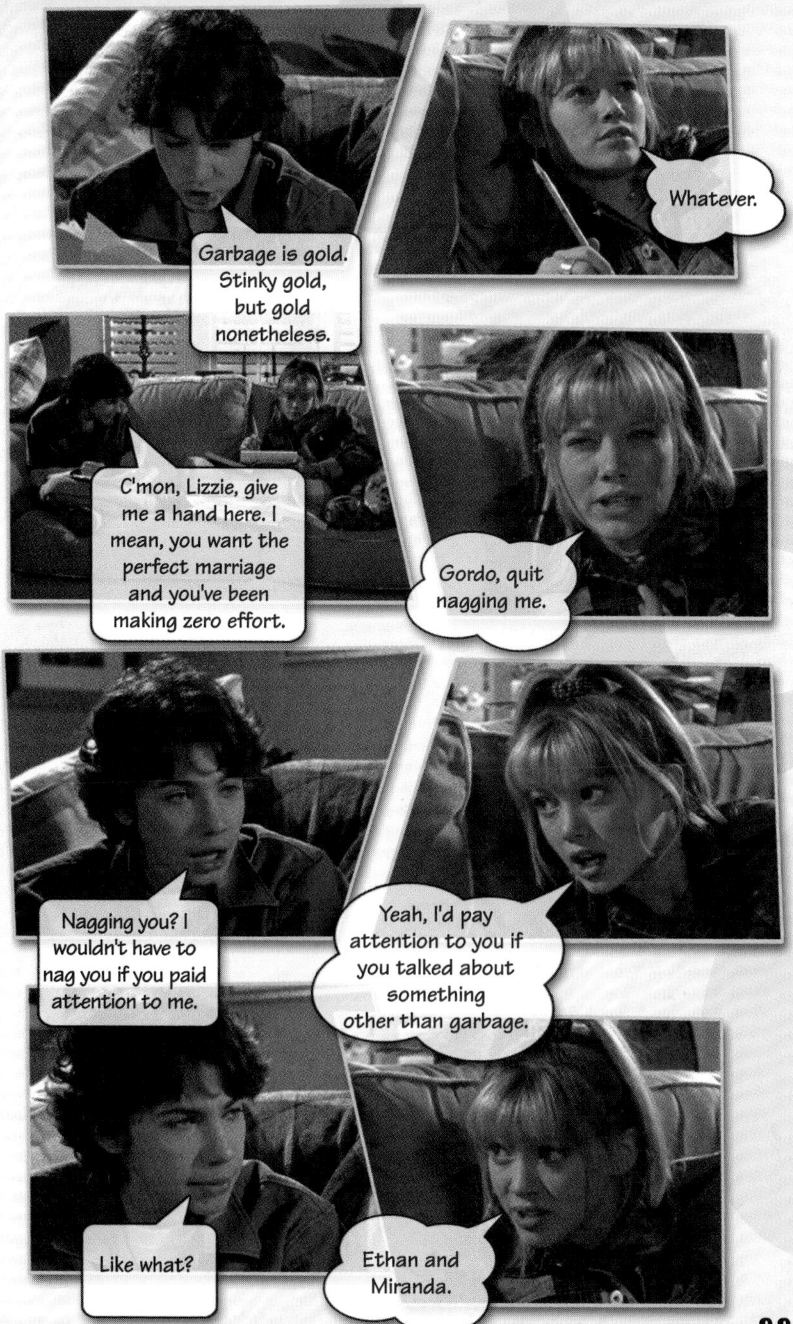
Garbage is gold. Stinky gold, but gold nonetheless.
Whatever.
C'mon, Lizzie, give me a hand here. I mean, you want the perfect marriage and you've been making zero effort.
Gordo, quit nagging me.
Nagging you? I wouldn't have to nag you if you paid attention to me.
Yeah, I'd pay attention to you if you talked about something other than garbage.
Like what?
Ethan and Miranda.

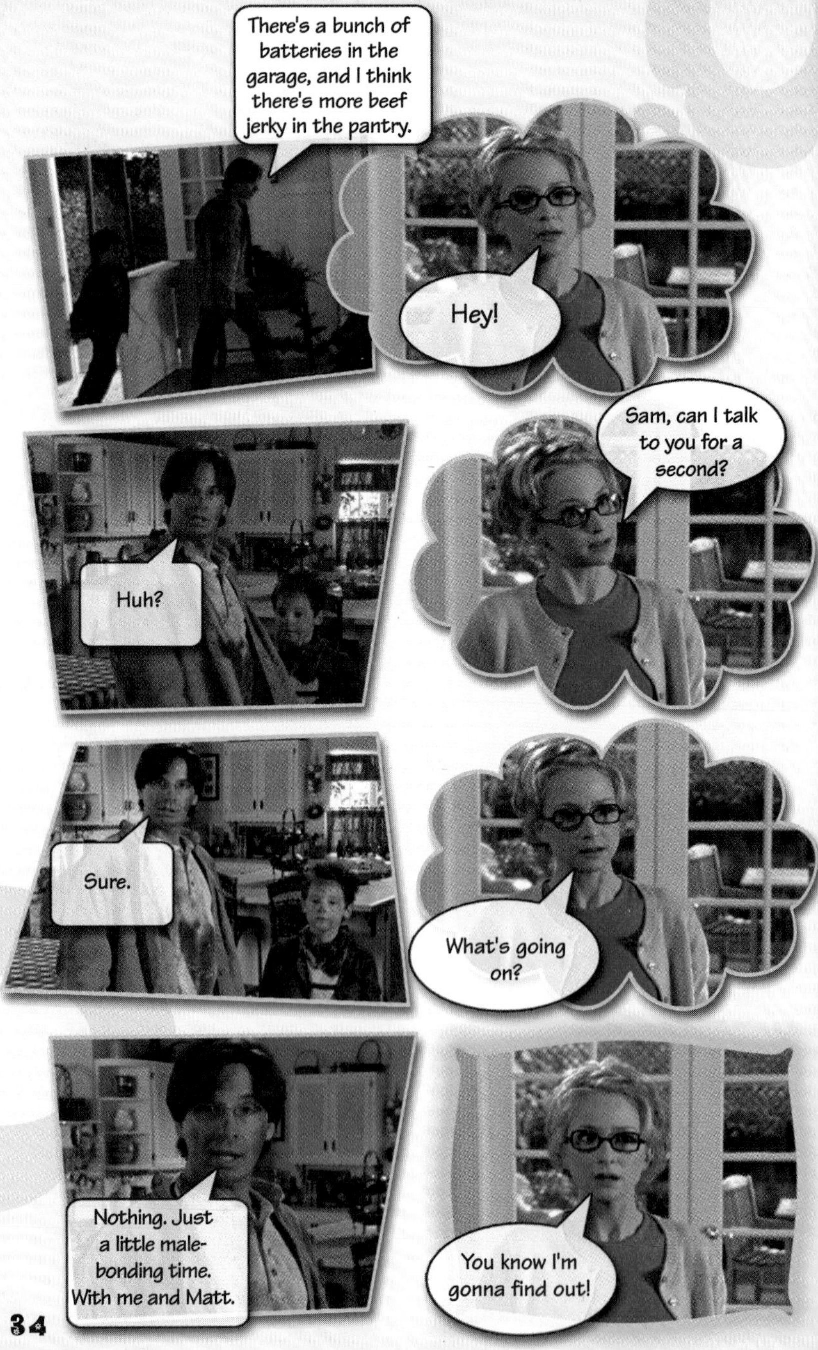
There's a bunch of batteries in the garage, and I think there's more beef jerky in the pantry.
Hey!
Sam, can I talk to you for a second?
Huh?
Sure.
What's going on?
Nothing. Just a little male-bonding time. With me and Matt.
You know I'm gonna find out!

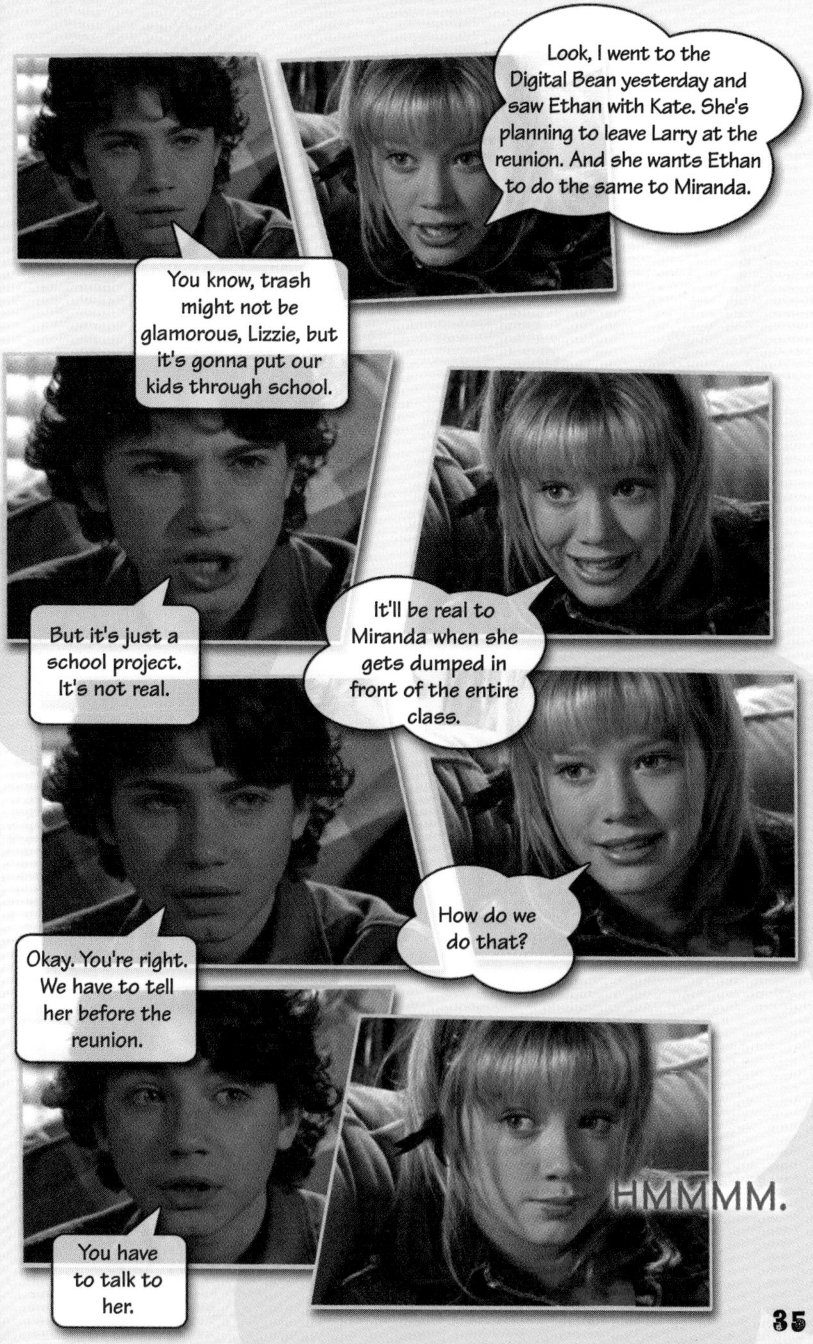
Look, I went to the Digital Bean yesterday and saw Ethan with Kate. She's planning to leave Larry at the reunion. And she wants Ethan to do the same to Miranda.
You know, trash might not be glamorous, Lizzie, but it's gonna put our kids through school.
But it's just a school project. It's not real.
It'll be real to Miranda when she gets dumped in front of the entire class.
Okay. You're right. We have to tell her before the reunion.
How do we do that?
You have to talk to her.
HMMMM.

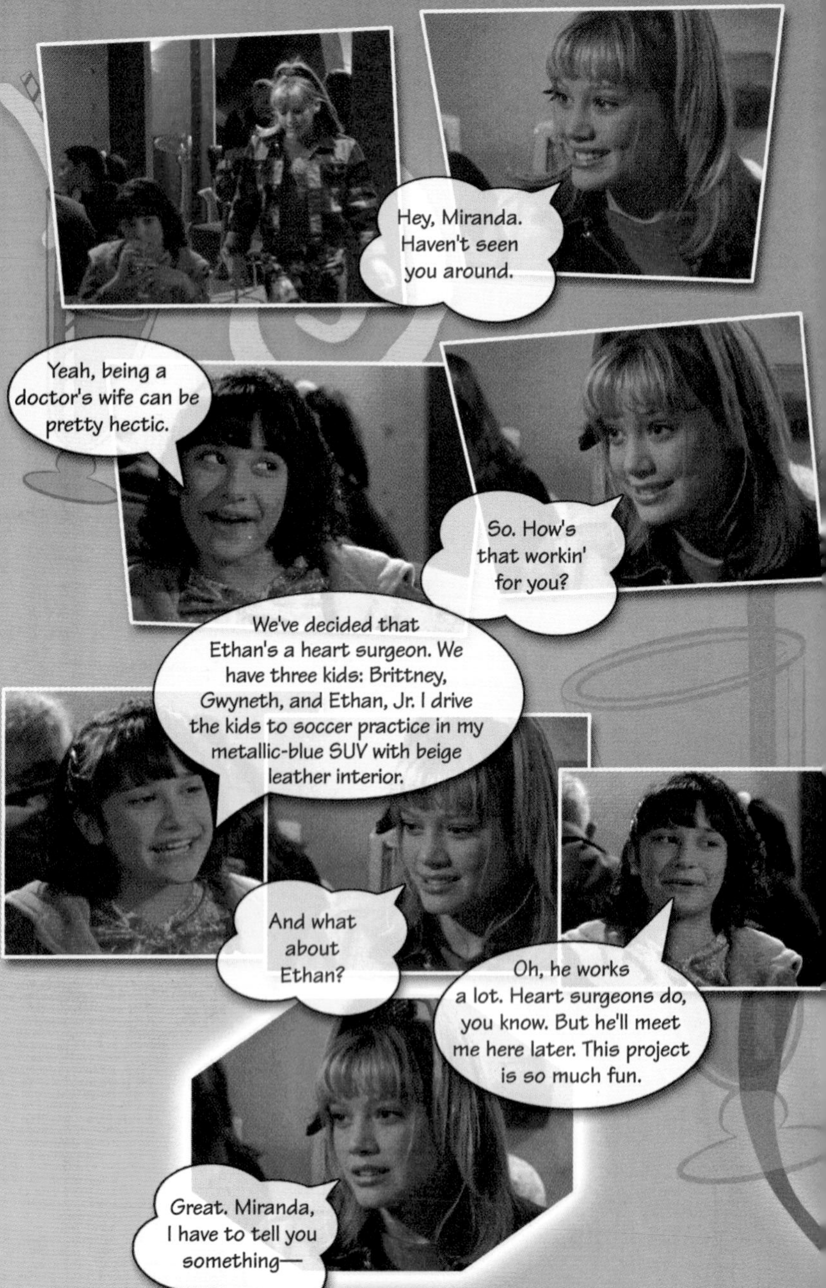

Hey, Miranda. Haven't seen you around.
Yeah, being a doctor's wife can be pretty hectic.
So. How's that workin' for you?
We've decided that Ethan's a heart surgeon. We have three kids: Brittney, Gwyneth, and Ethan, Jr. I drive the kids to soccer practice in my metallic-blue SUV with beige leather interior.
And what about Ethan?
Oh, he works a lot. Heart surgeons do, you know. But he'll meet me here later. This project is so much fun.
Great. Miranda, I have to tell you something—

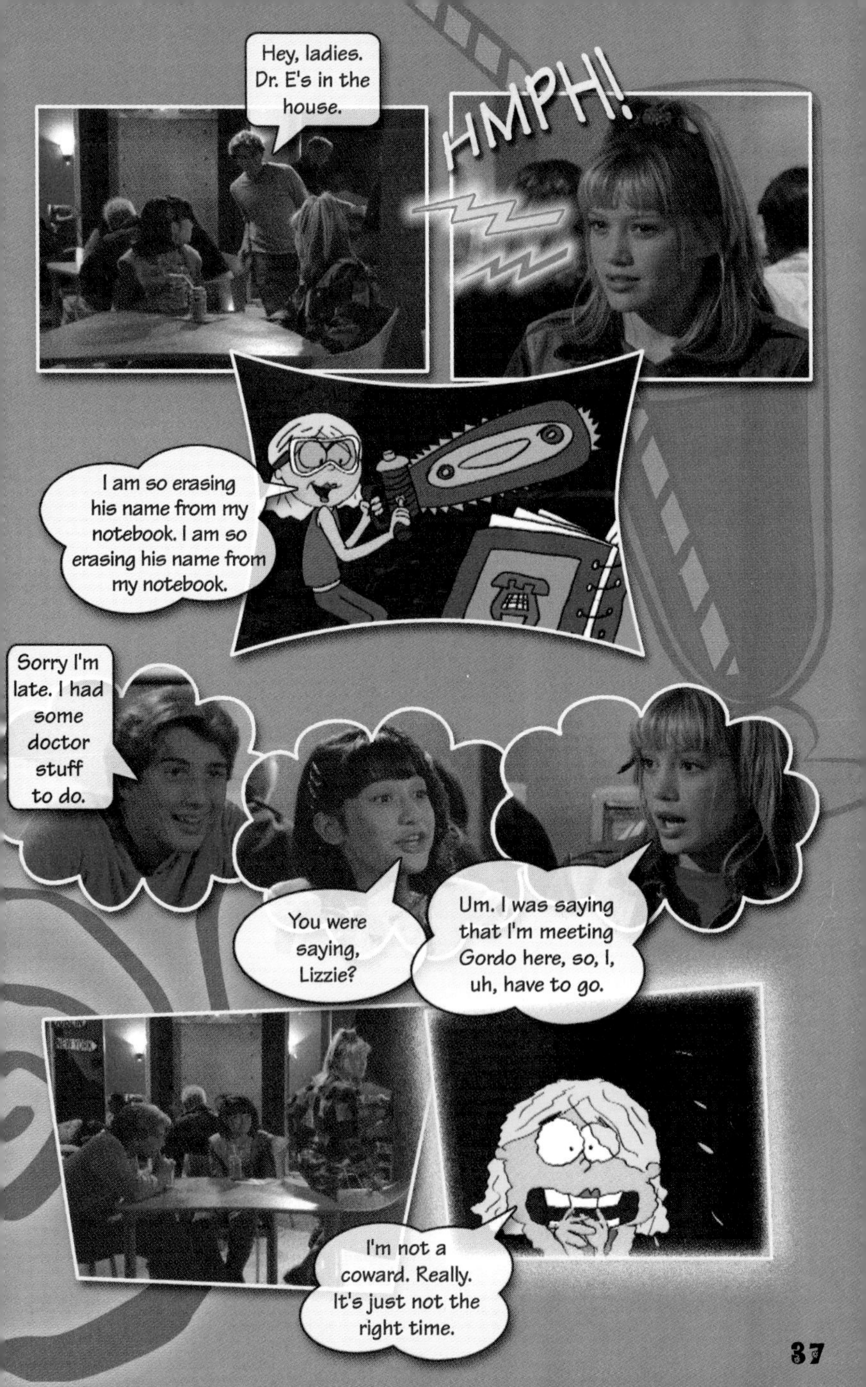
Hey, ladies. Dr. E's in the house.
HMPH!
I am so erasing his name from my notebook. I am so erasing his name from my notebook.
Sorry I'm late. I had some doctor stuff to do.
You were saying, Lizzie?
Um. I was saying that I'm meeting Gordo here, so, I, uh, have to go.
I'm not a coward. Really. It's just not the right time.

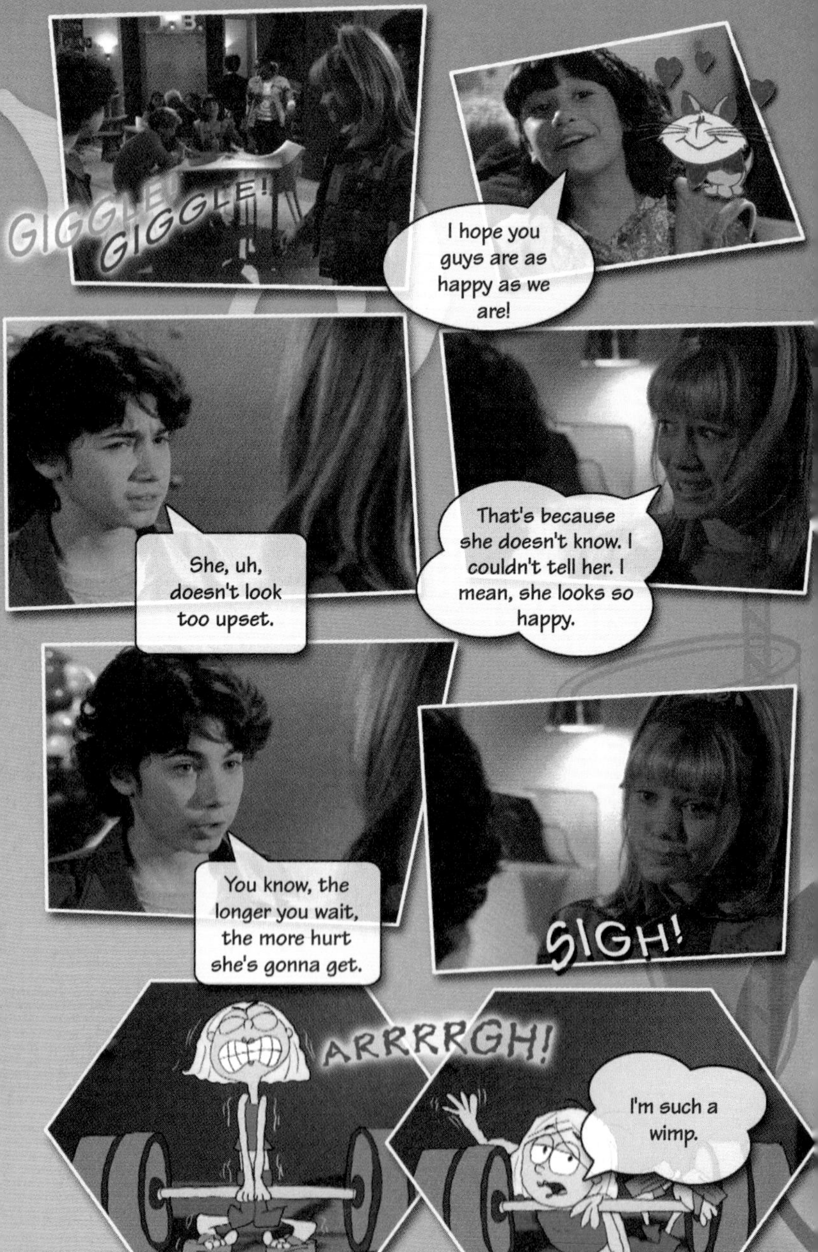
GIGGLE! GIGGLE!
I hope you guys are as happy as we are!
She, uh, doesn't look too upset.
That's because she doesn't know. I couldn't tell her. I mean, she looks so happy.
You know, the longer you wait, the more hurt she's gonna get.
SIGH!
ARRRRGH!
I'm such a wimp.

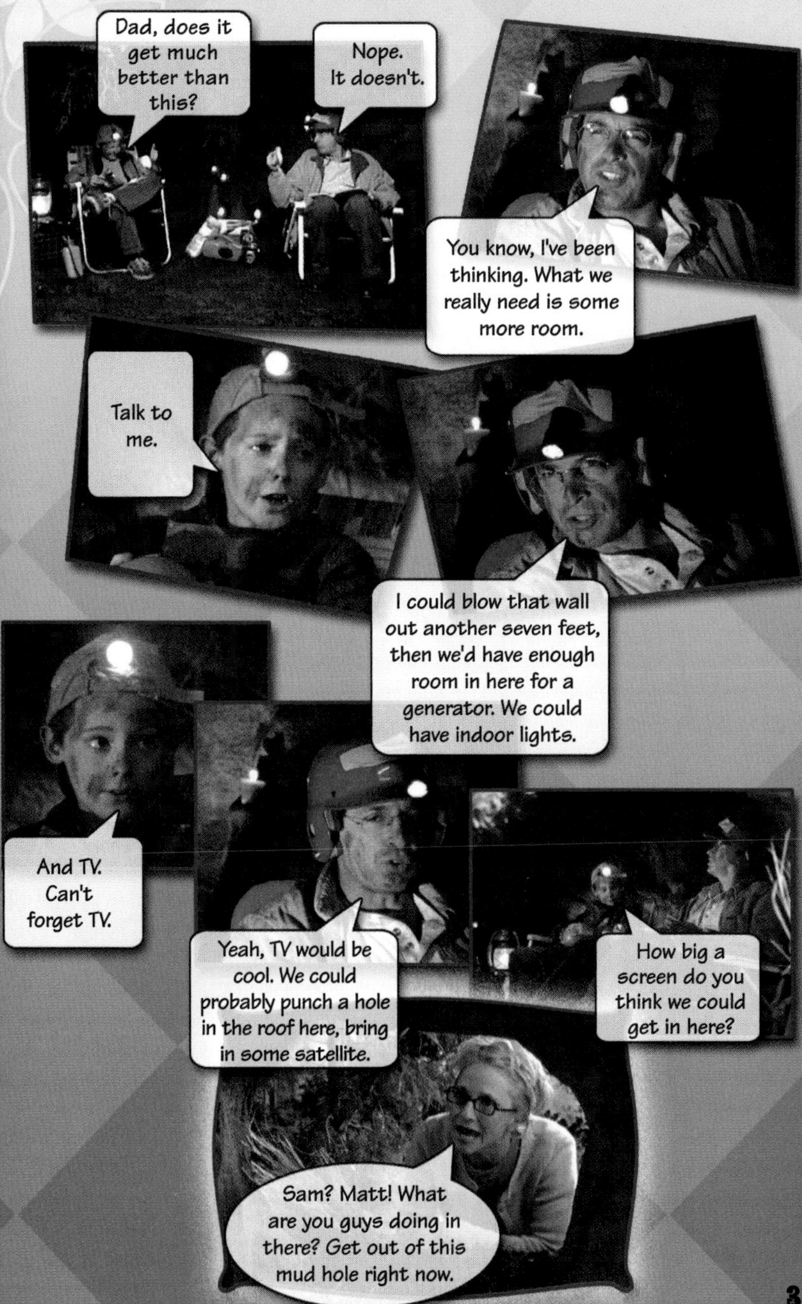

Dad, does it get much better than this?
Nope. It doesn't.
You know, I've been thinking. What we really need is some more room.
Talk to me.
I could blow that wall out another seven feet, then we'd have enough room in here for a generator. We could have indoor lights.
And TV. Can't forget TV.
Yeah, TV would be cool. We could probably punch a hole in the roof here, bring in some satellite.
How big a screen do you think we could get in here?
Sam? Matt! What are you guys doing in there? Get out of this mud hole right now.

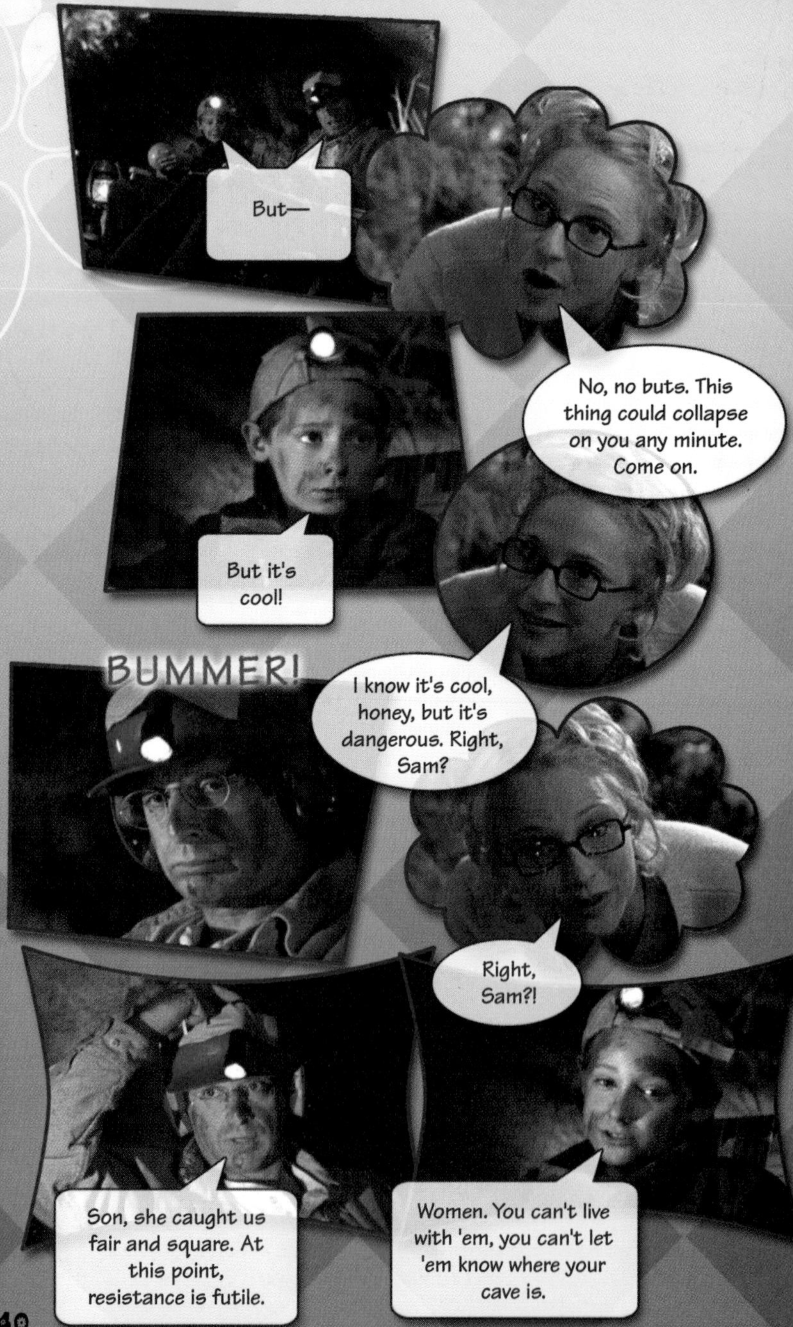
But—
No, no buts. This thing could collapse on you any minute. Come on.
But it's cool!
I know it's cool, honey, but it's dangerous. Right, Sam?
BUMMER!
Right, Sam?!
Son, she caught us fair and square. At this point, resistance is futile.
Women. You can't live with 'em, you can't let 'em know where your cave is.

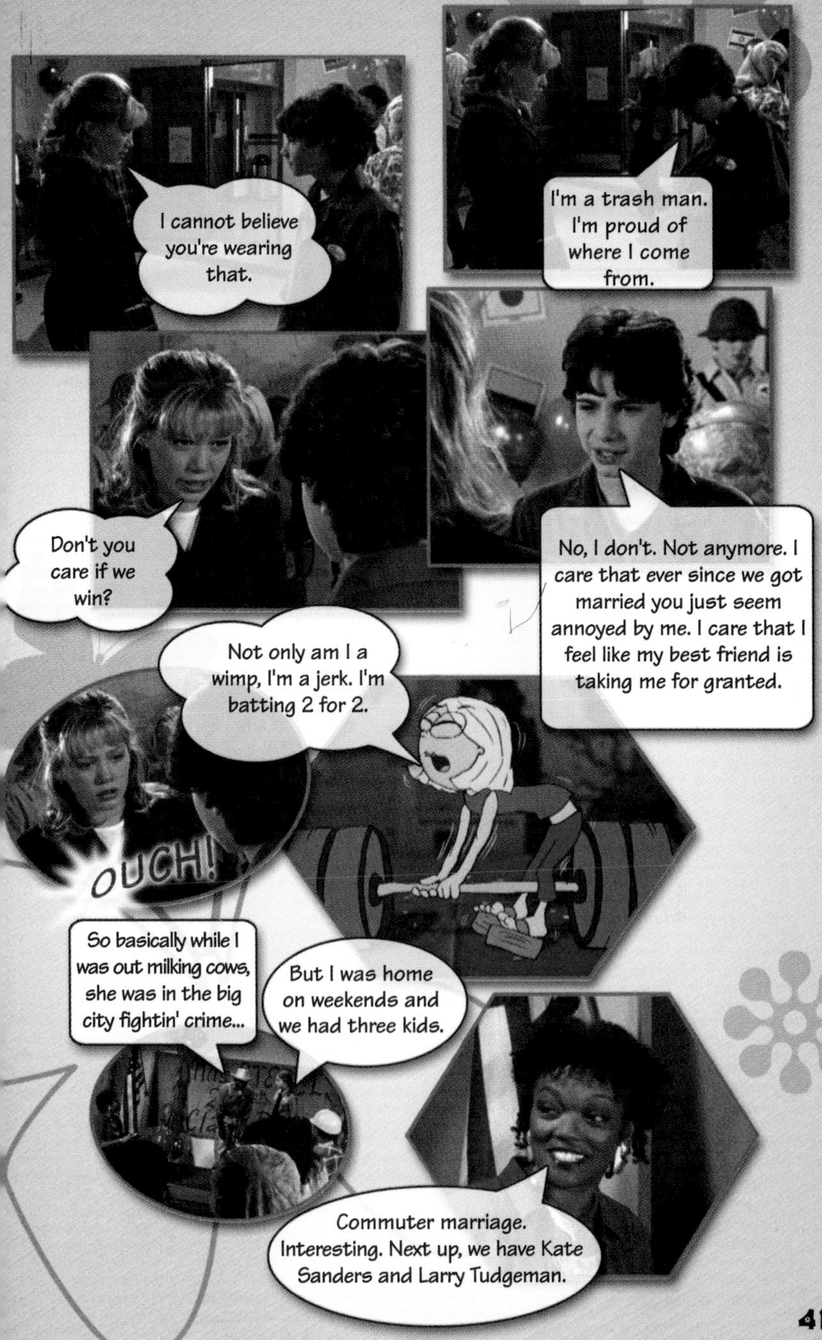

I cannot believe you're wearing that.
I'm a trash man. I'm proud of where I come from.
Don't you care if we win?
No, I don't. Not anymore. I care that ever since we got married you just seem annoyed by me. I care that I feel like my best friend is taking me for granted.
Not only am I a wimp, I'm a jerk. I'm batting 2 for 2.
OUCH!
So basically while I was out milking cows, she was in the big city fightin' crime...
But I was home on weekends and we had three kids.
Commuter marriage. Interesting. Next up, we have Kate Sanders and Larry Tudgeman.

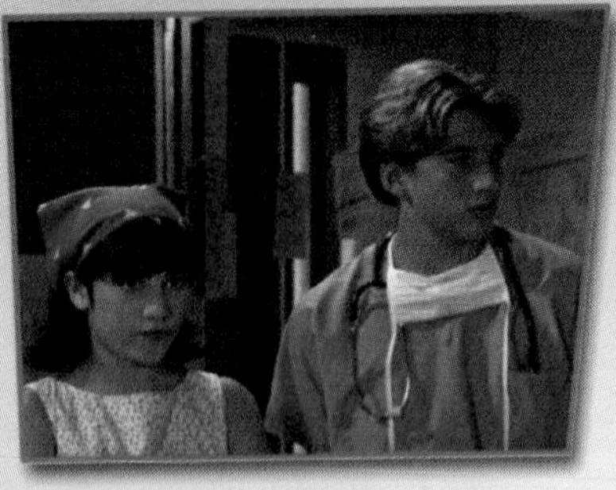

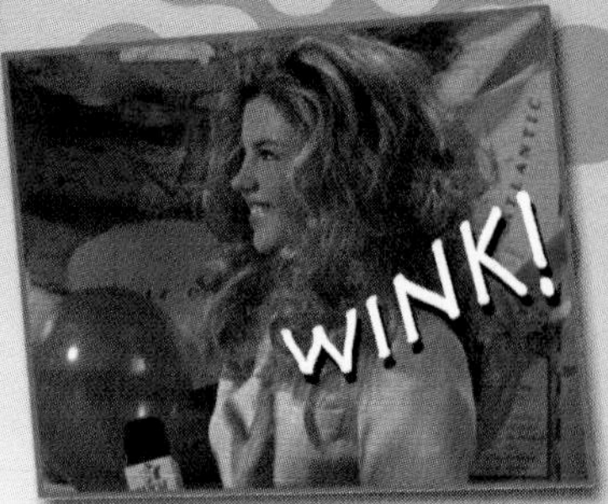
WINK!

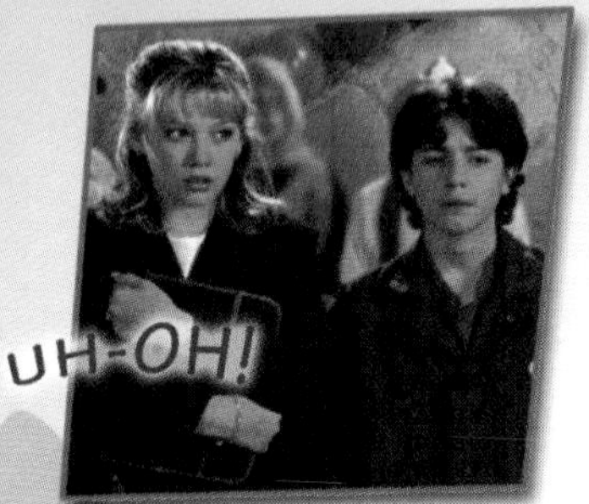
UH-OH!

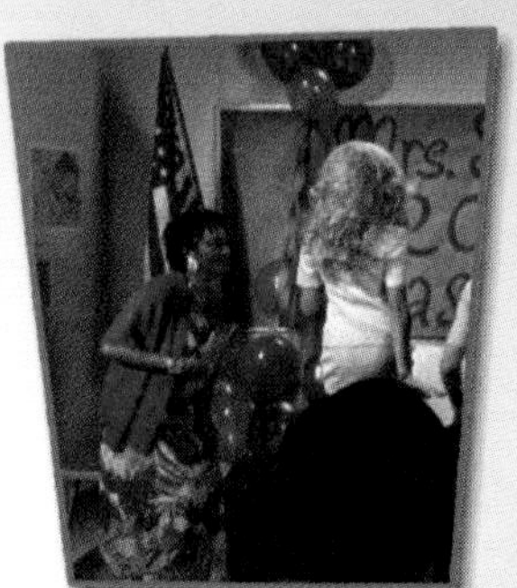

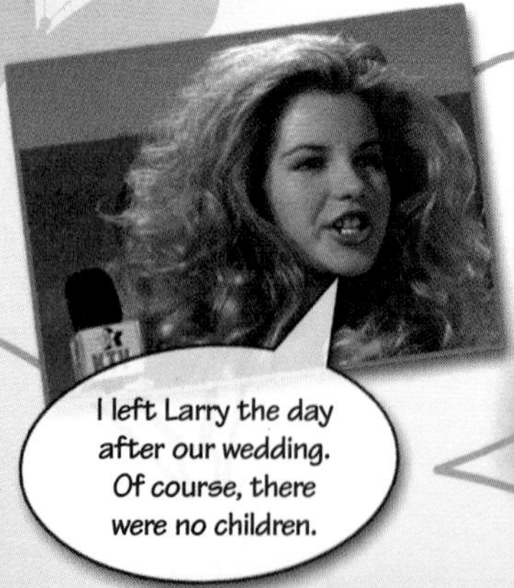
I left Larry the day
after our wedding.
Of course, there
were no children.

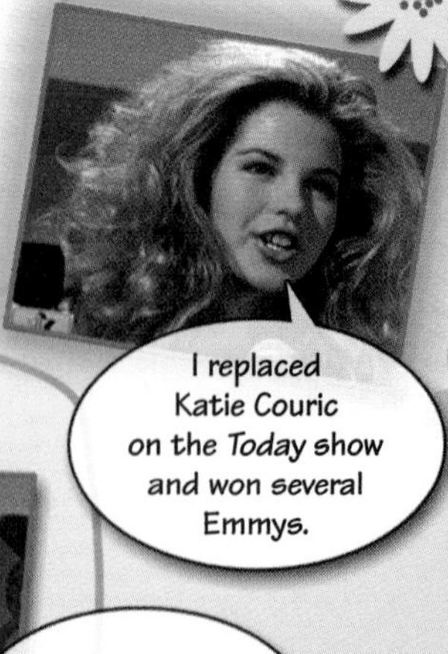
I replaced
Katie Couric
on the *Today* show
and won several
Emmys.

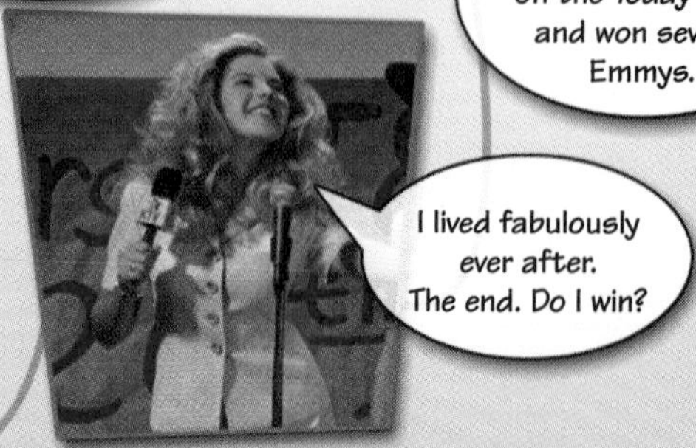
I lived fabulously
ever after.
The end. Do I win?

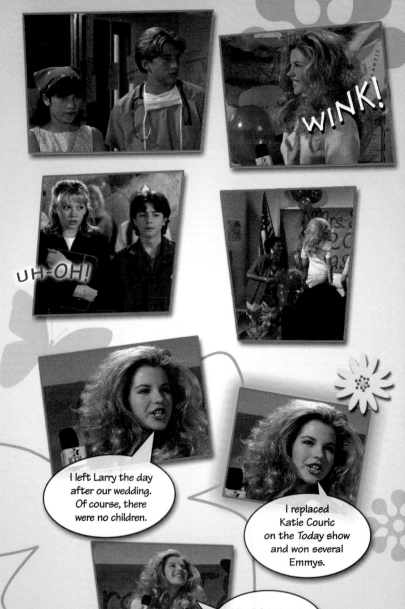

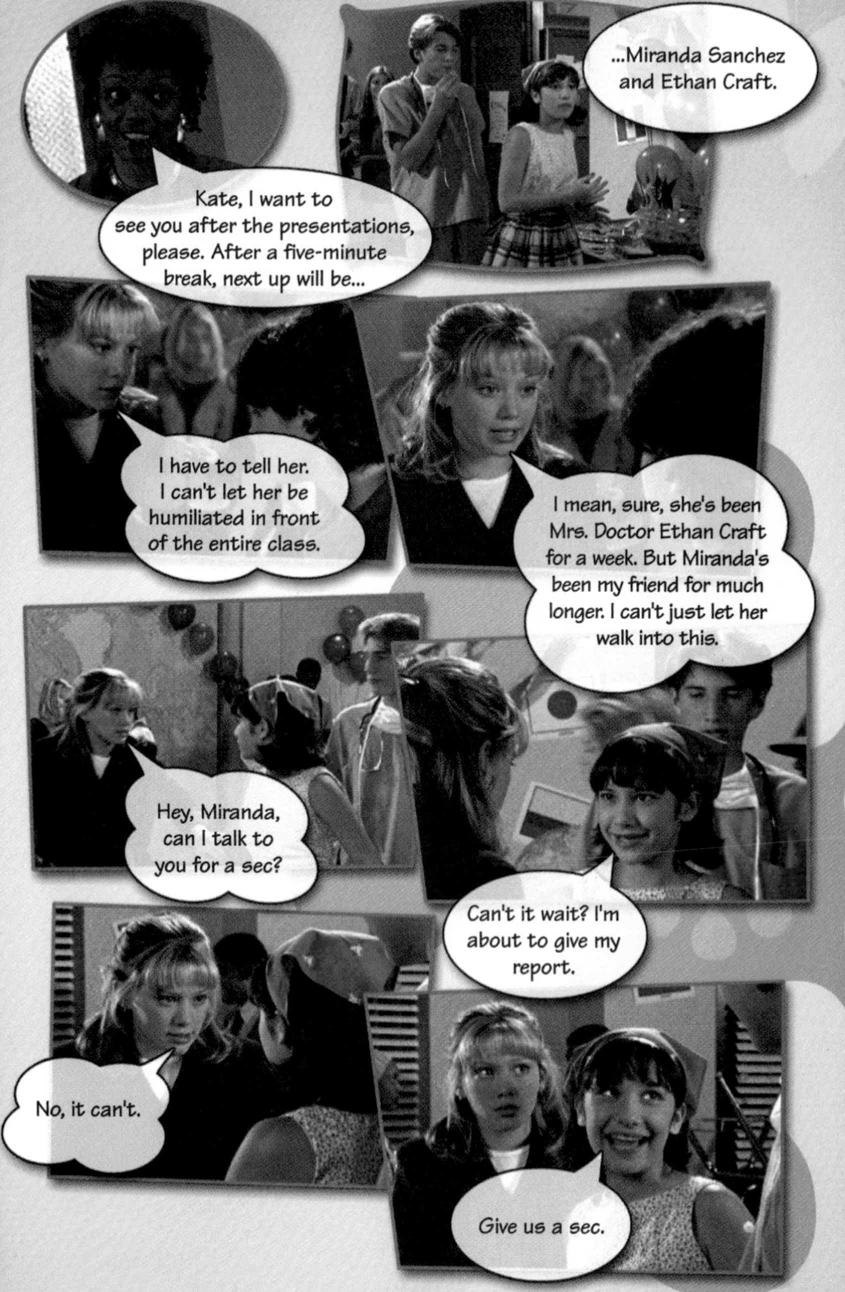
...Miranda Sanchez and Ethan Craft.
Kate, I want to see you after the presentations, please. After a five-minute break, next up will be...
I have to tell her. I can't let her be humiliated in front of the entire class.
I mean, sure, she's been Mrs. Doctor Ethan Craft for a week. But Miranda's been my friend for much longer. I can't just let her walk into this.
Hey, Miranda, can I talk to you for a sec?
Can't it wait? I'm about to give my report.
No, it can't.
Give us a sec.

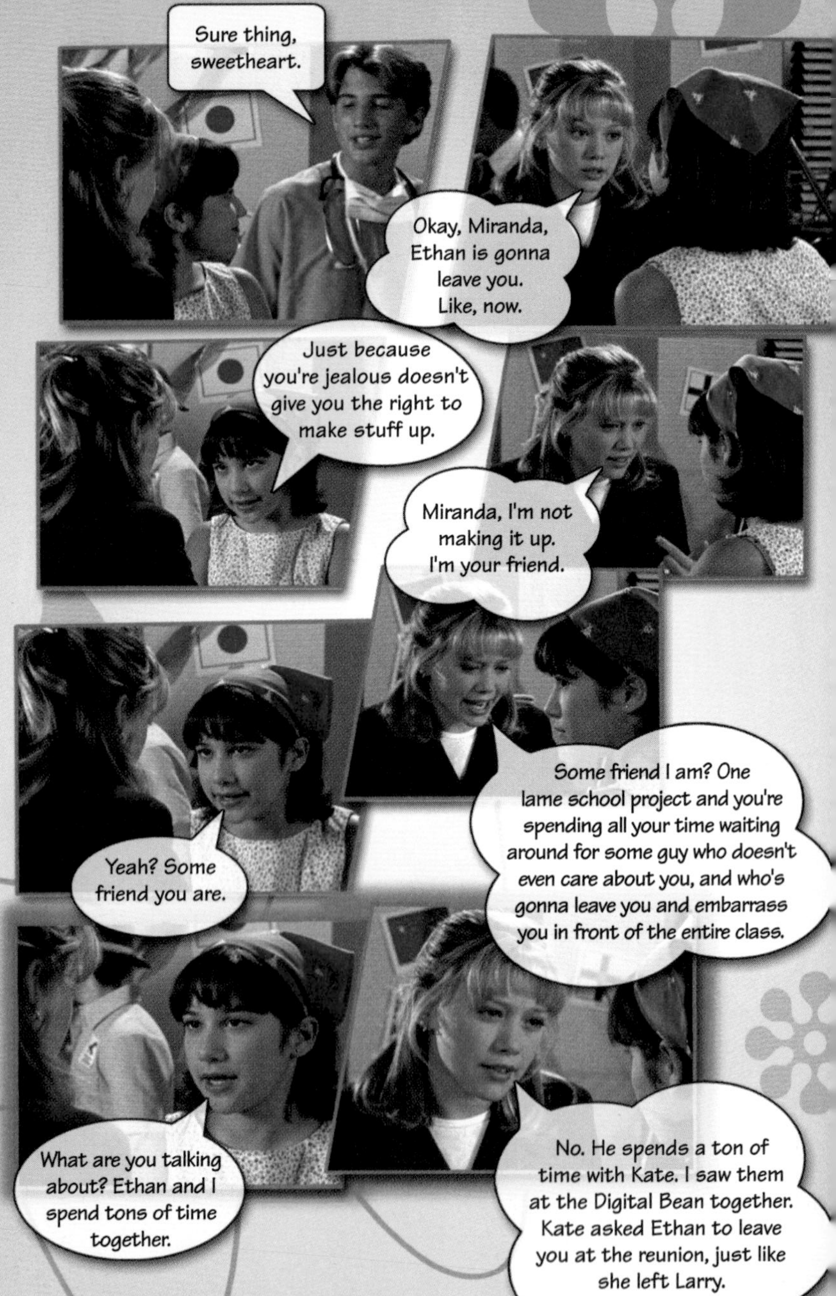
Sure thing, sweetheart.
Okay, Miranda, Ethan is gonna leave you. Like, now.
Just because you're jealous doesn't give you the right to make stuff up.
Miranda, I'm not making it up. I'm your friend.
Yeah? Some friend you are.
Some friend I am? One lame school project and you're spending all your time waiting around for some guy who doesn't even care about you, and who's gonna leave you and embarrass you in front of the entire class.
What are you talking about? Ethan and I spend tons of time together.
No. He spends a ton of time with Kate. I saw them at the Digital Bean together. Kate asked Ethan to leave you at the reunion, just like she left Larry.

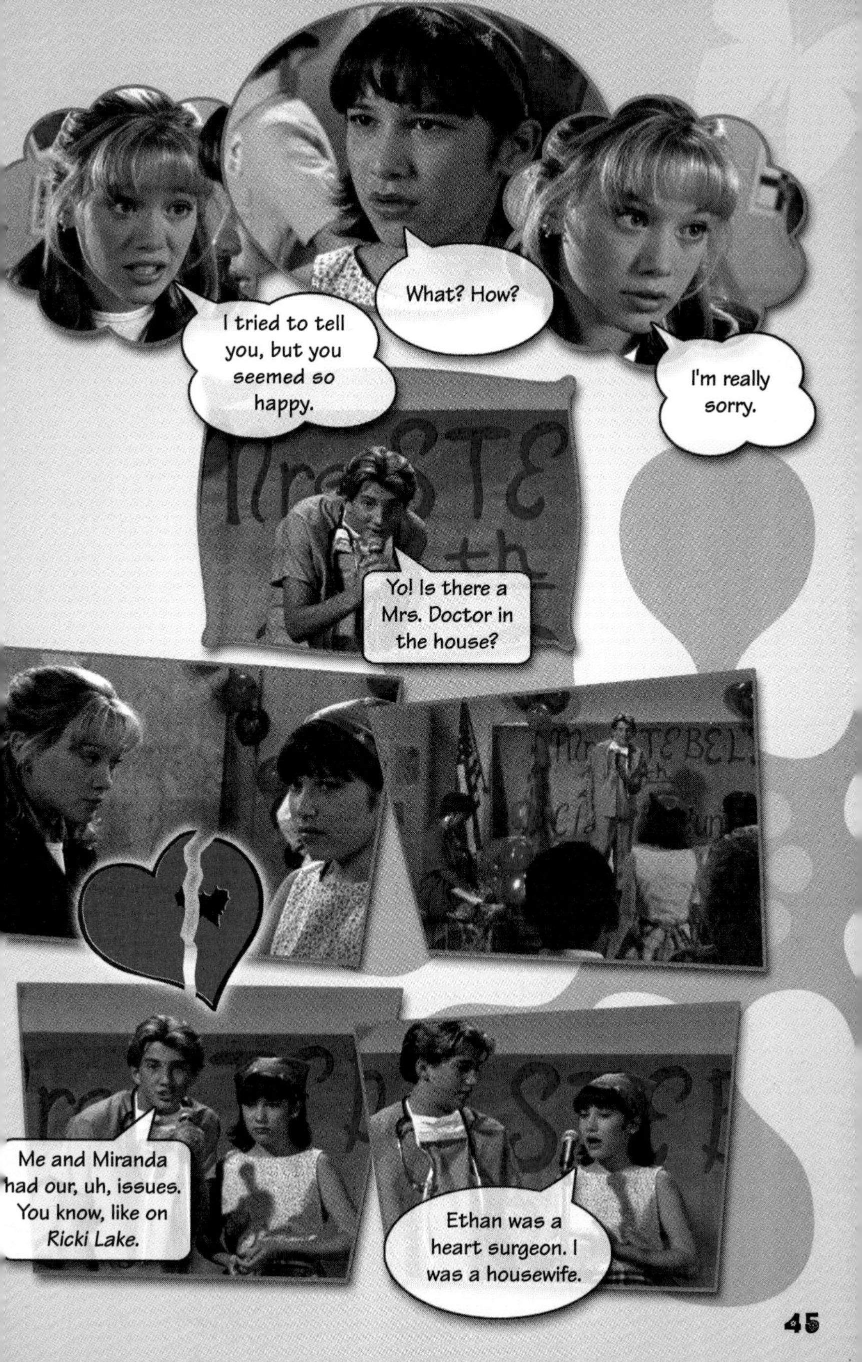
I tried to tell you, but you seemed so happy.
What? How?
I'm really sorry.
Yo! Is there a Mrs. Doctor in the house?
Me and Miranda had our, uh, issues. You know, like on *Ricki Lake.*
Ethan was a heart surgeon. I was a housewife.

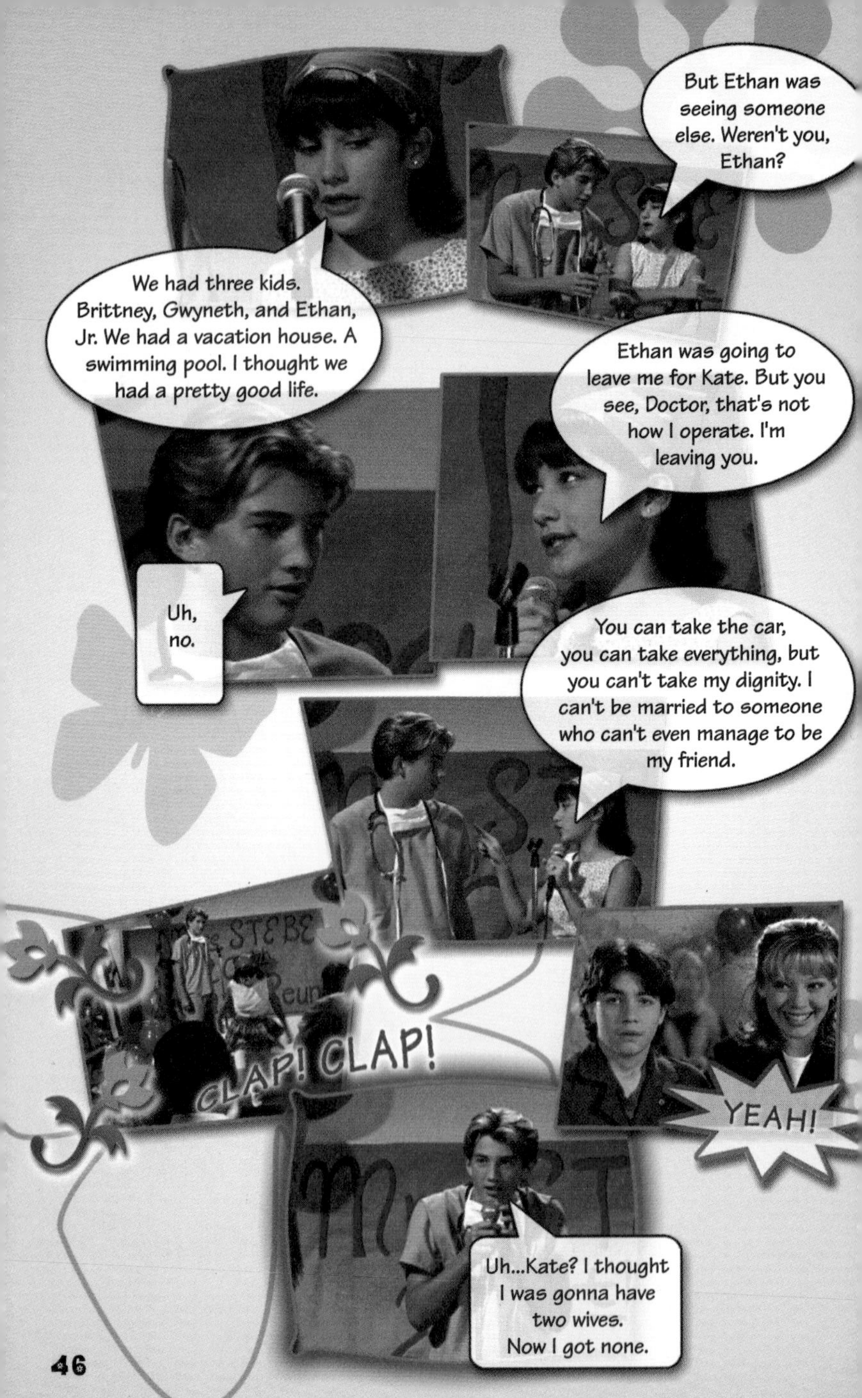
We had three kids. Brittney, Gwyneth, and Ethan, Jr. We had a vacation house. A swimming pool. I thought we had a pretty good life.
But Ethan was seeing someone else. Weren't you, Ethan?
Uh, no.
Ethan was going to leave me for Kate. But you see, Doctor, that's not how I operate. I'm leaving you.
You can take the car, you can take everything, but you can't take my dignity. I can't be married to someone who can't even manage to be my friend.
CLAP! CLAP!
YEAH!
Uh...Kate? I thought I was gonna have two wives. Now I got none.

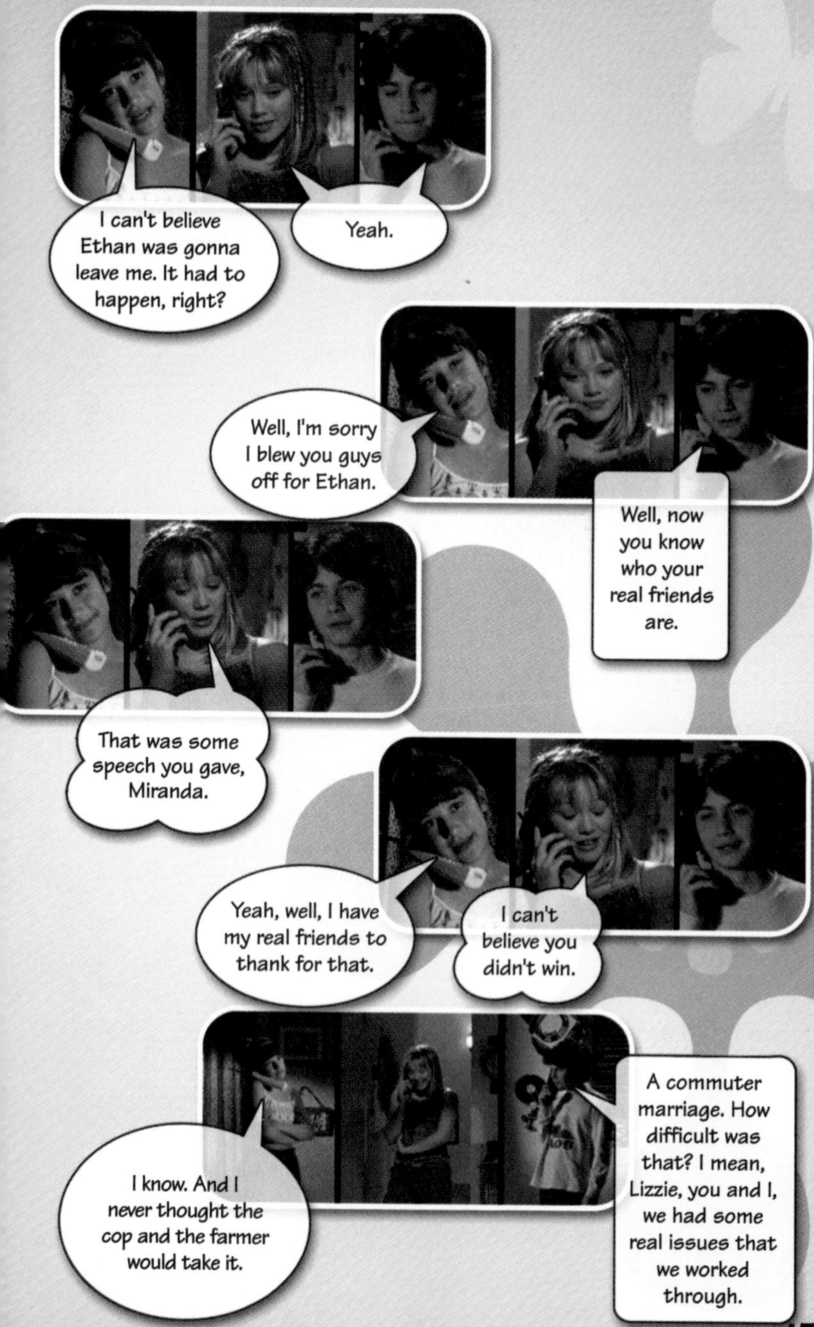
I can't believe Ethan was gonna leave me. It had to happen, right?
Yeah.
Well, I'm sorry I blew you guys off for Ethan.
Well, now you know who your real friends are.
That was some speech you gave, Miranda.
Yeah, well, I have my real friends to thank for that.
I can't believe you didn't win.
I know. And I never thought the cop and the farmer would take it.
A commuter marriage. How difficult was that? I mean, Lizzie, you and I, we had some real issues that we worked through.

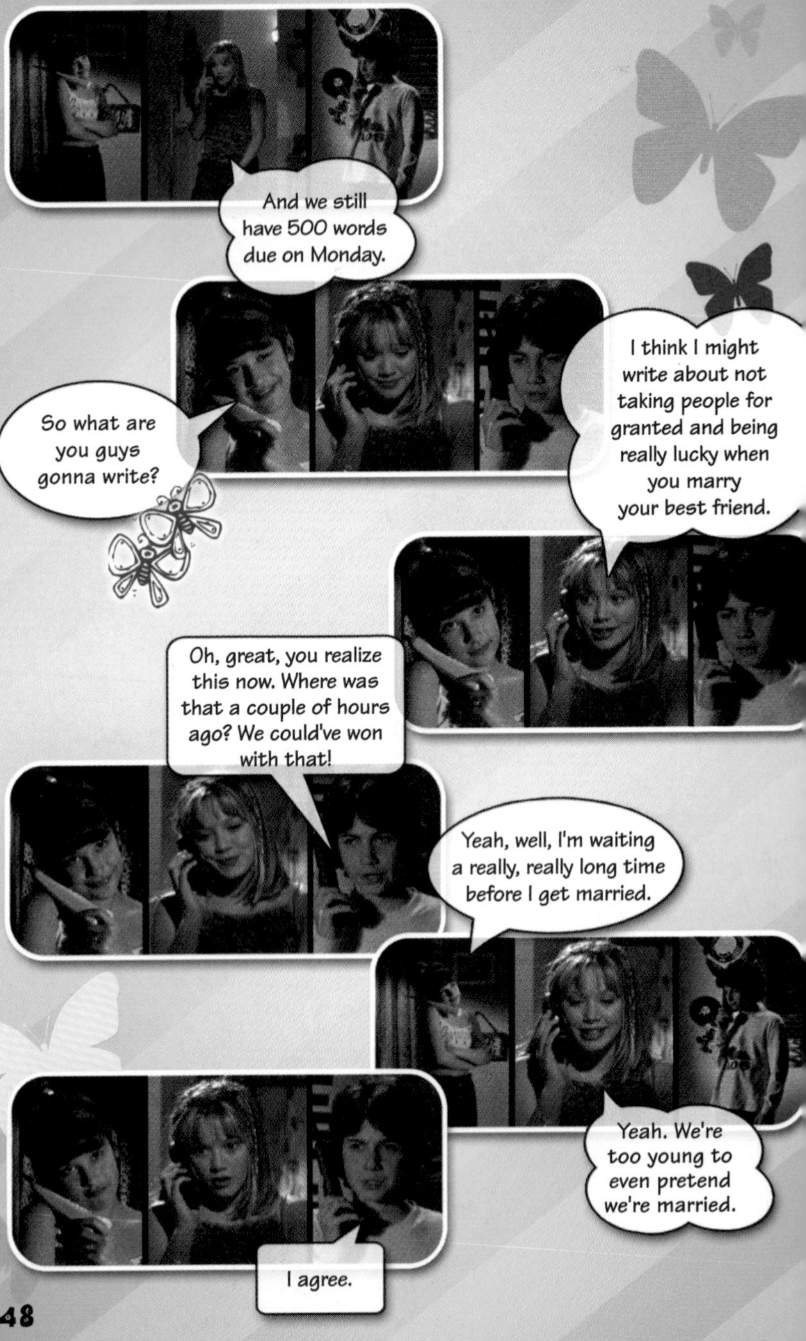
And we still have 500 words due on Monday.
So what are you guys gonna write?
I think I might write about not taking people for granted and being really lucky when you marry your best friend.
Oh, great, you realize this now. Where was that a couple of hours ago? We could've won with that!
Yeah, well, I'm waiting a really, really long time before I get married.
Yeah. We're too young to even pretend we're married.
I agree.

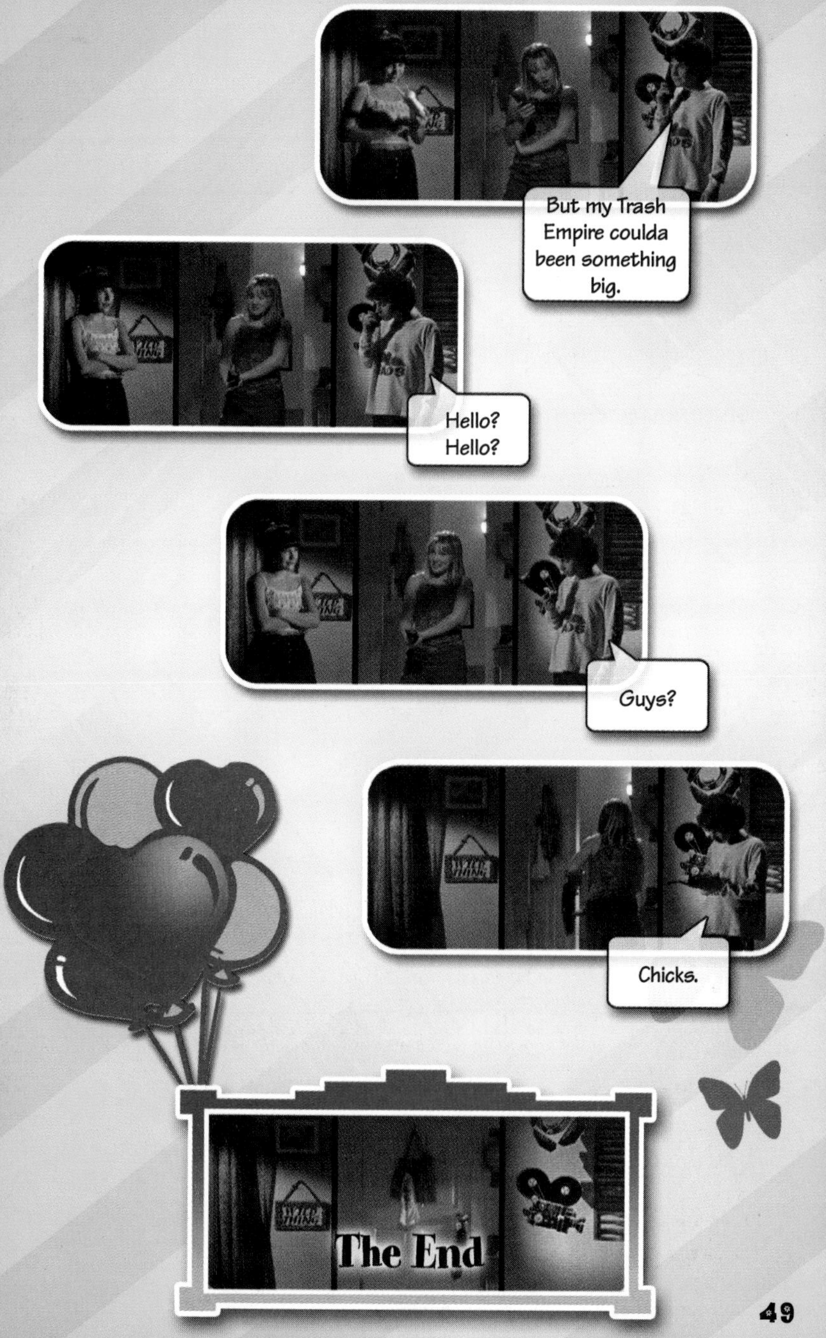
But my Trash Empire coulda been something big.
Hello? Hello?
Guys?
Chicks.
The End

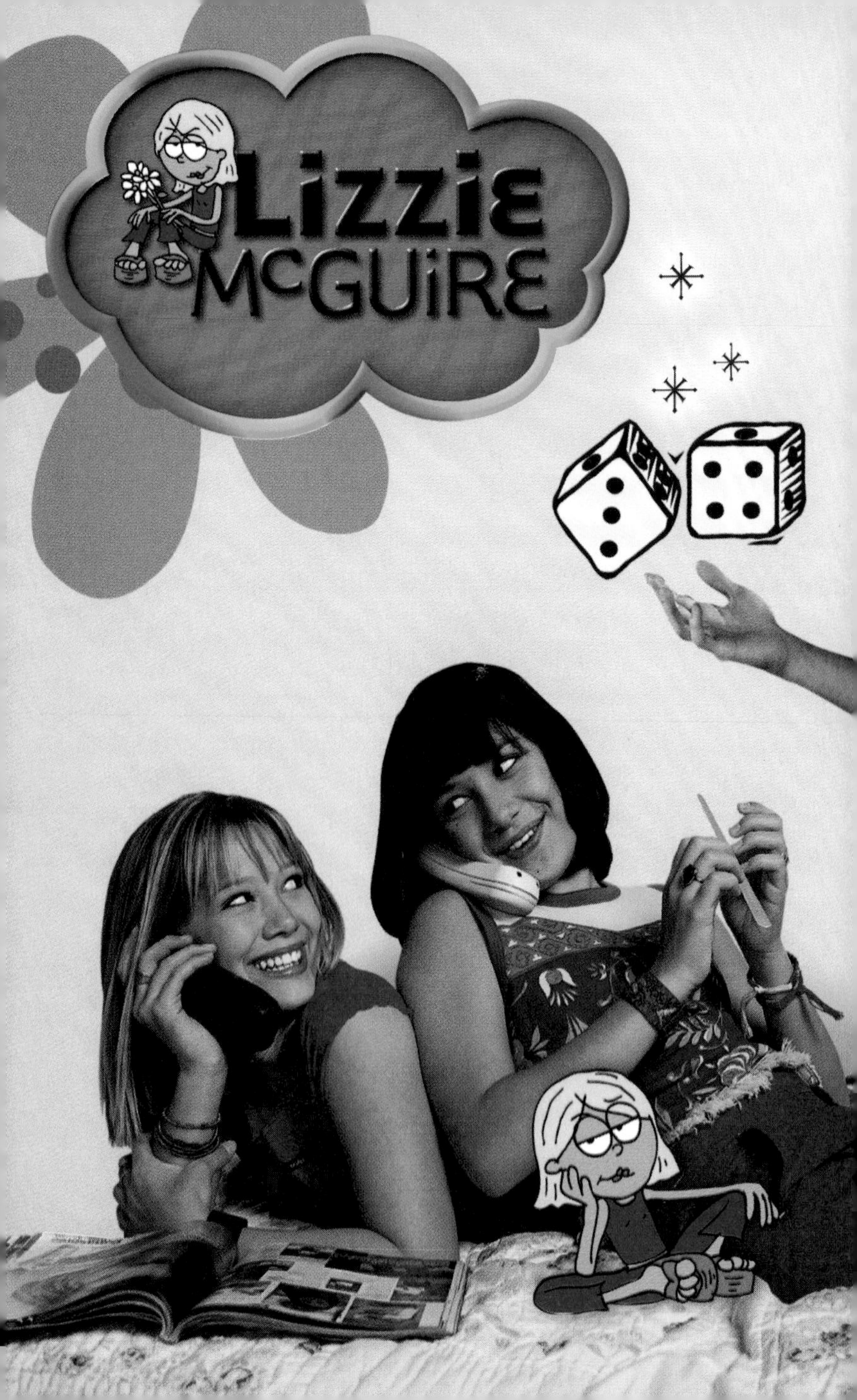
Lizzie
McGUIRE

Episode 8

"Come Fly With Me"

Gordo introduces Lizzie and Miranda to lounge culture, accidentally starting the hottest fad ever! But when everyone else jumps on the Las Vegas bandwagon, it's the trendsetter himself who's left behind.

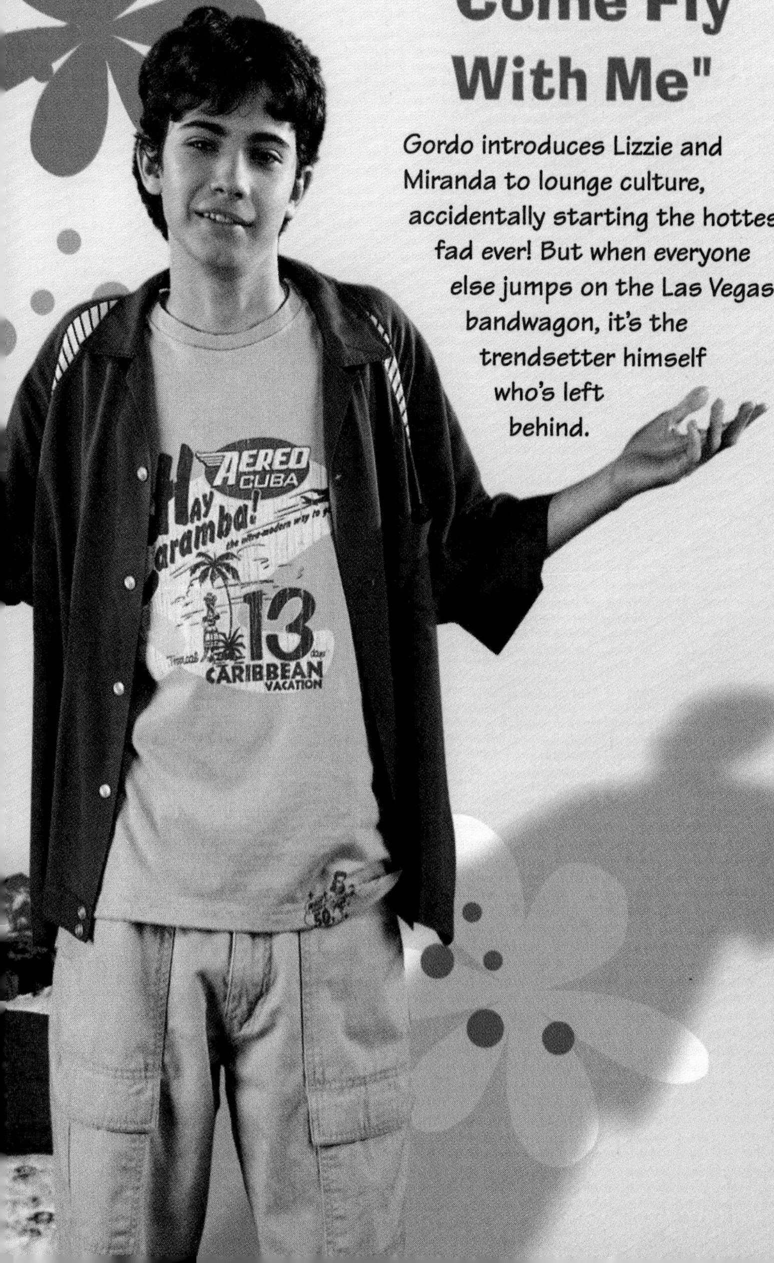
AEREO
CUBA
13
CARIBBEAN
VACATION

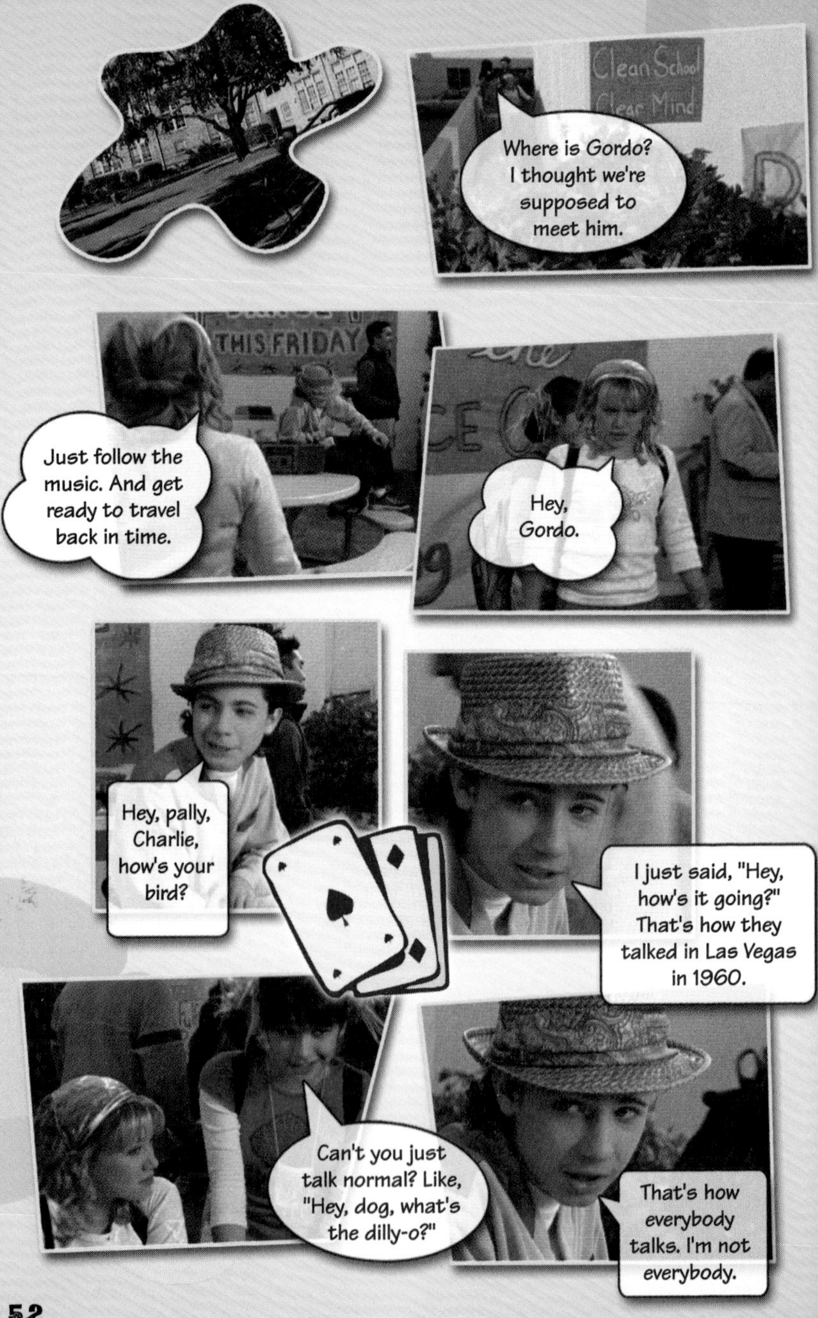
Clean School
Clear Mind
Where is Gordo? I thought we're supposed to meet him.
THIS FRIDAY
Just follow the music. And get ready to travel back in time.
Hey, Gordo.
Hey, pally, Charlie, how's your bird?
I just said, "Hey, how's it going?" That's how they talked in Las Vegas in 1960.
Can't you just talk normal? Like, "Hey, dog, what's the dilly-o?"
That's how everybody talks. I'm not everybody.

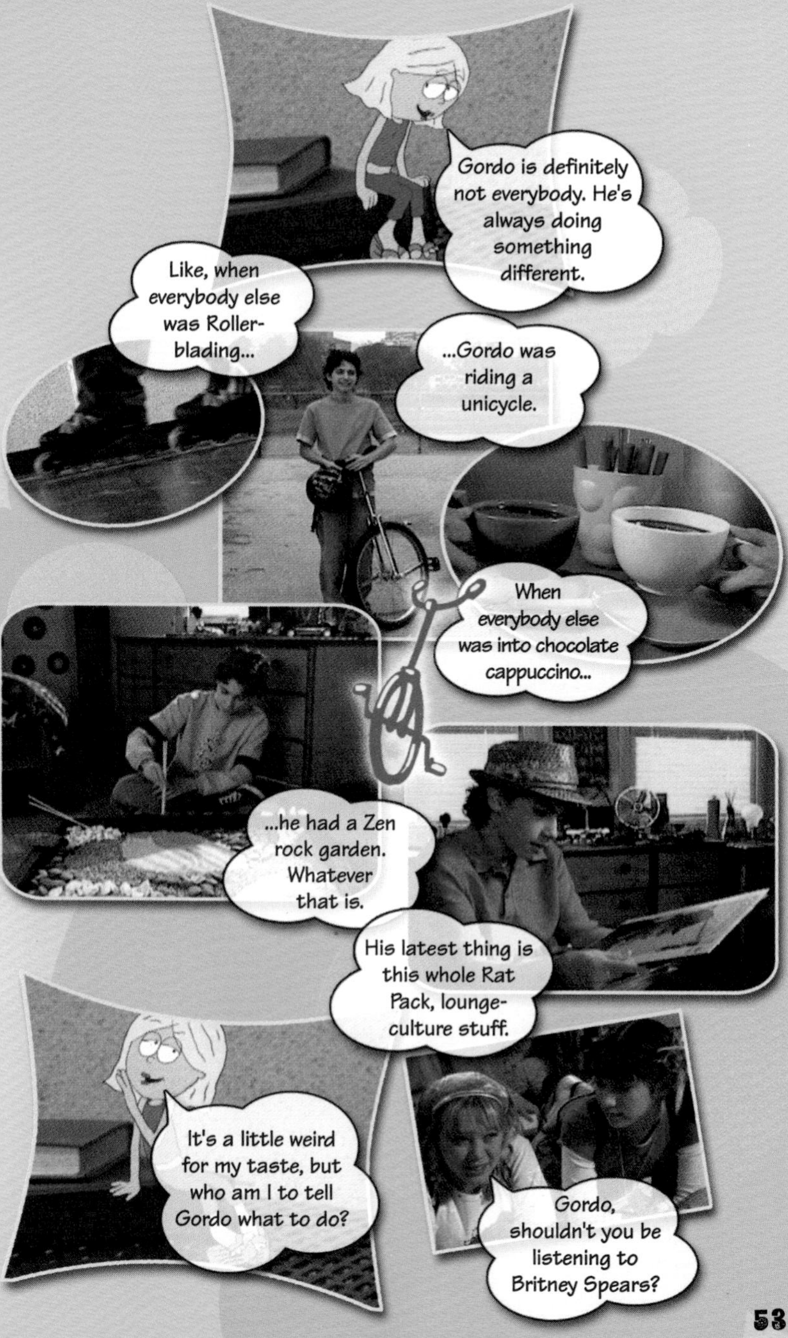

Gordo is definitely not everybody. He's always doing something different.
Like, when everybody else was Roller-blading...
...Gordo was riding a unicycle.
When everybody else was into chocolate cappuccino...
...he had a Zen rock garden. Whatever that is.
His latest thing is this whole Rat Pack, lounge-culture stuff.
It's a little weird for my taste, but who am I to tell Gordo what to do?
Gordo, shouldn't you be listening to Britney Spears?

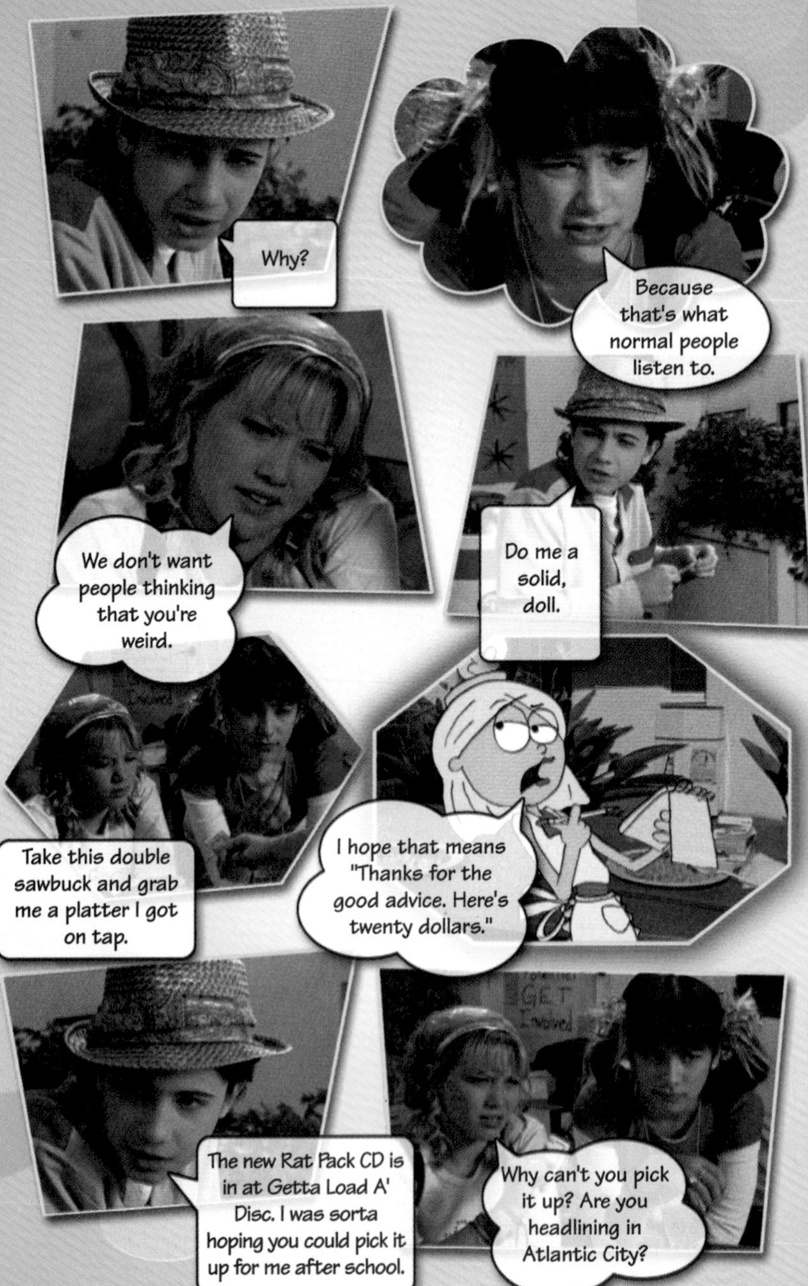
Why?
Because that's what normal people listen to.
We don't want people thinking that you're weird.
Do me a solid, doll.
Take this double sawbuck and grab me a platter I got on tap.
I hope that means "Thanks for the good advice. Here's twenty dollars."
The new Rat Pack CD is in at Getta Load A' Disc. I was sorta hoping you could pick it up for me after school.
Why can't you pick it up? Are you headlining in Atlantic City?

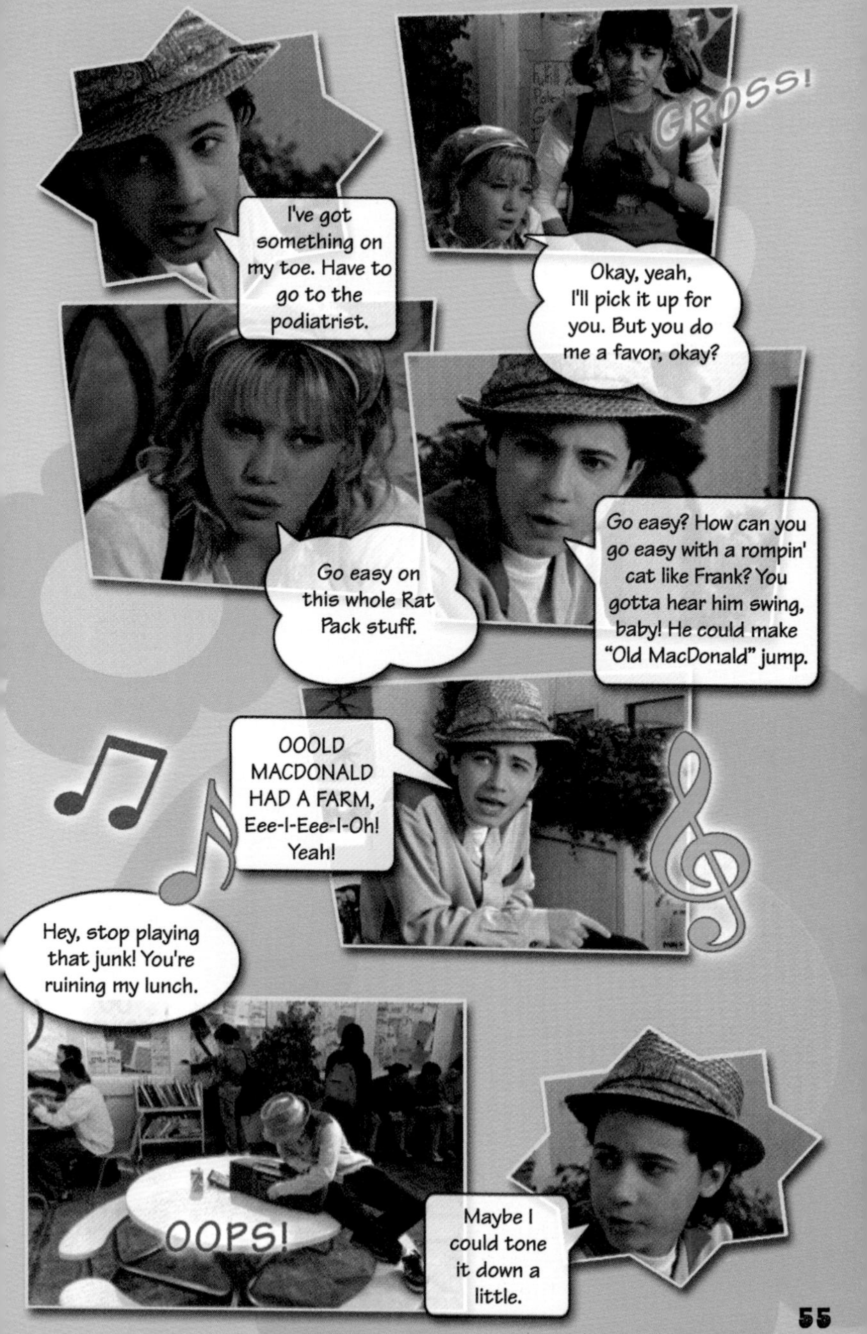

I've got something on my toe. Have to go to the podiatrist.
GROSS!
Okay, yeah, I'll pick it up for you. But you do me a favor, okay?
Go easy on this whole Rat Pack stuff.
Go easy? How can you go easy with a rompin' cat like Frank? You gotta hear him swing, baby! He could make "Old MacDonald" jump.
OOOLD MACDONALD HAD A FARM, Eee-I-Eee-I-Oh! Yeah!
Hey, stop playing that junk! You're ruining my lunch.
OOPS!
Maybe I could tone it down a little.

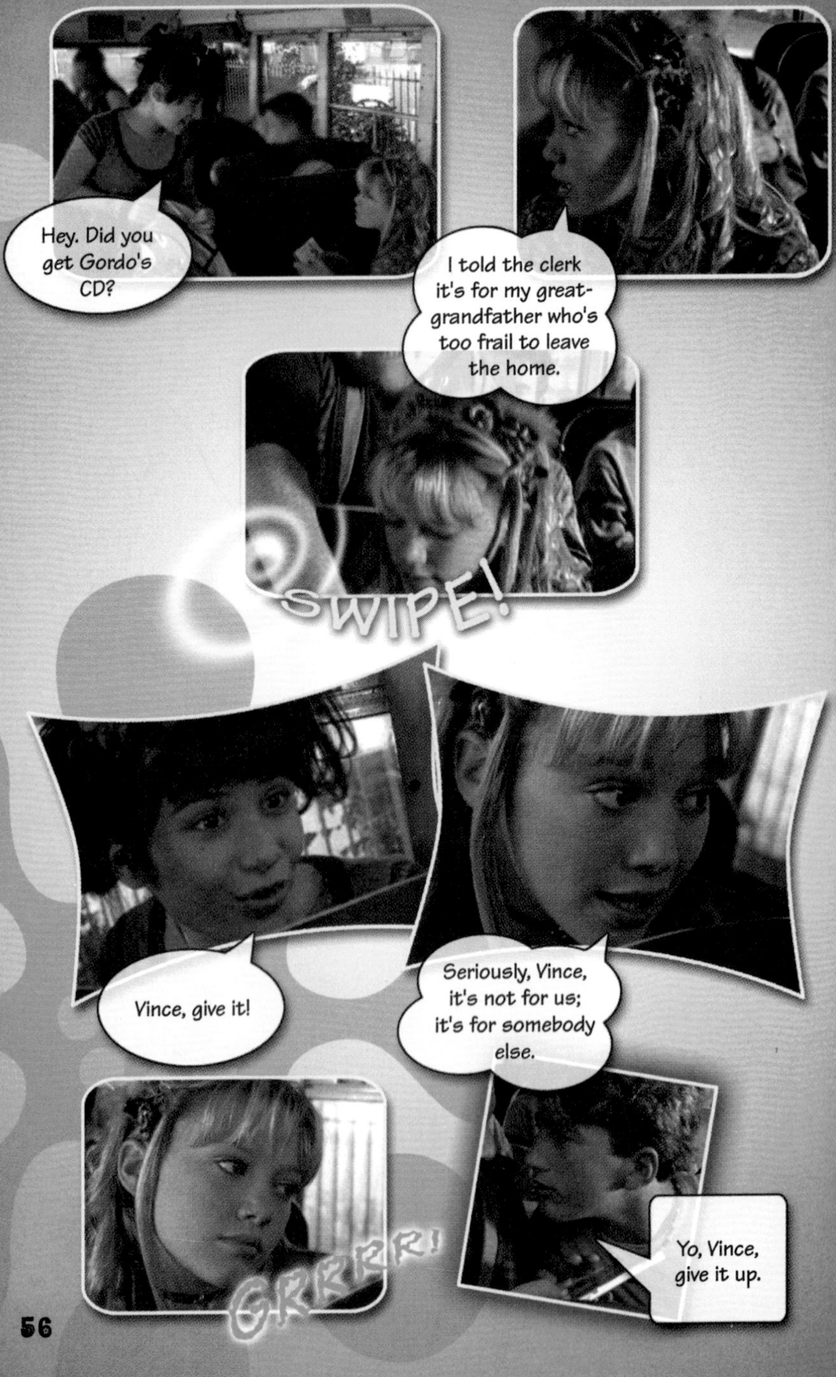
Hey. Did you get Gordo's CD?
I told the clerk it's for my great-grandfather who's too frail to leave the home.
SWIPE!
Vince, give it!
Seriously, Vince, it's not for us; it's for somebody else.
GRRRR!
Yo, Vince, give it up.

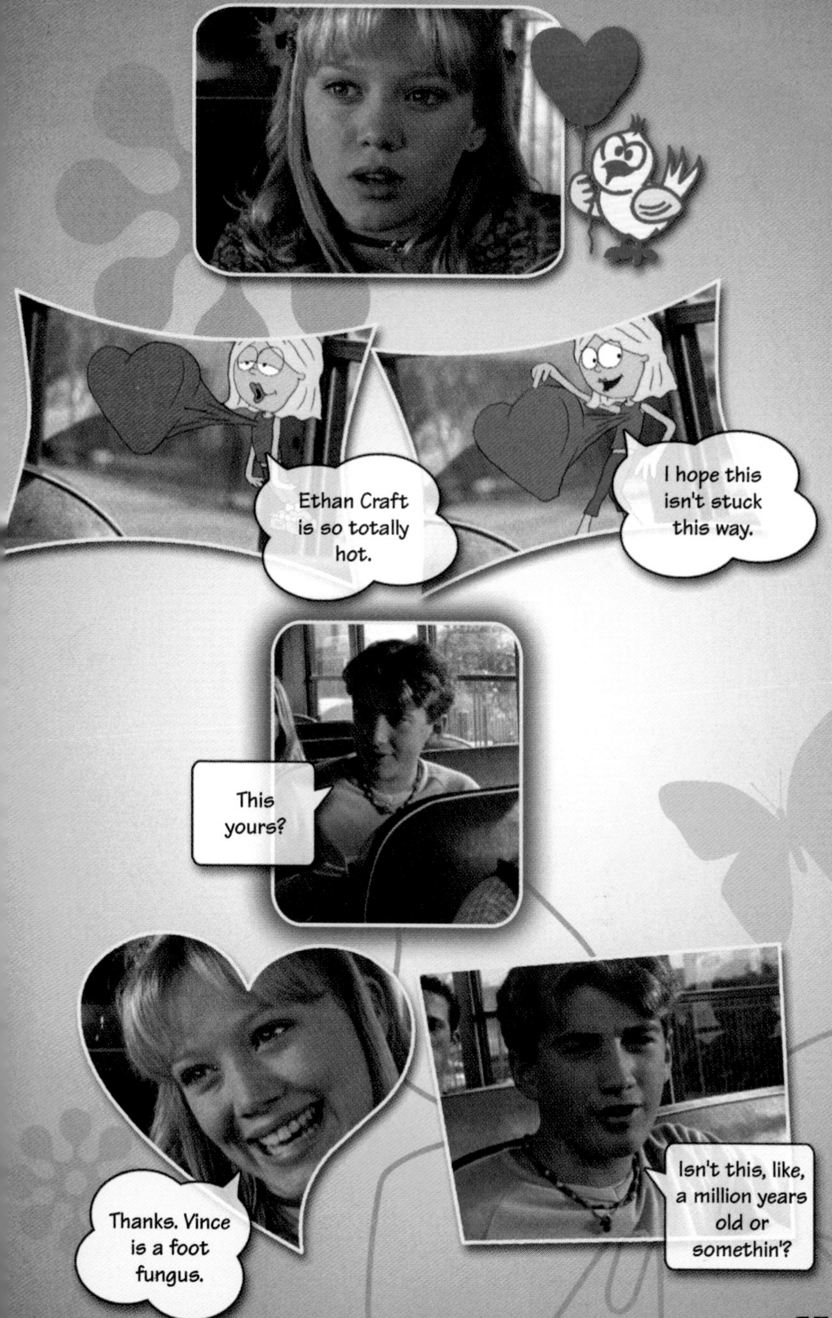
Ethan Craft is so totally hot.
I hope this isn't stuck this way.
This yours?
Thanks. Vince is a foot fungus.
Isn't this, like, a million years old or somethin'?

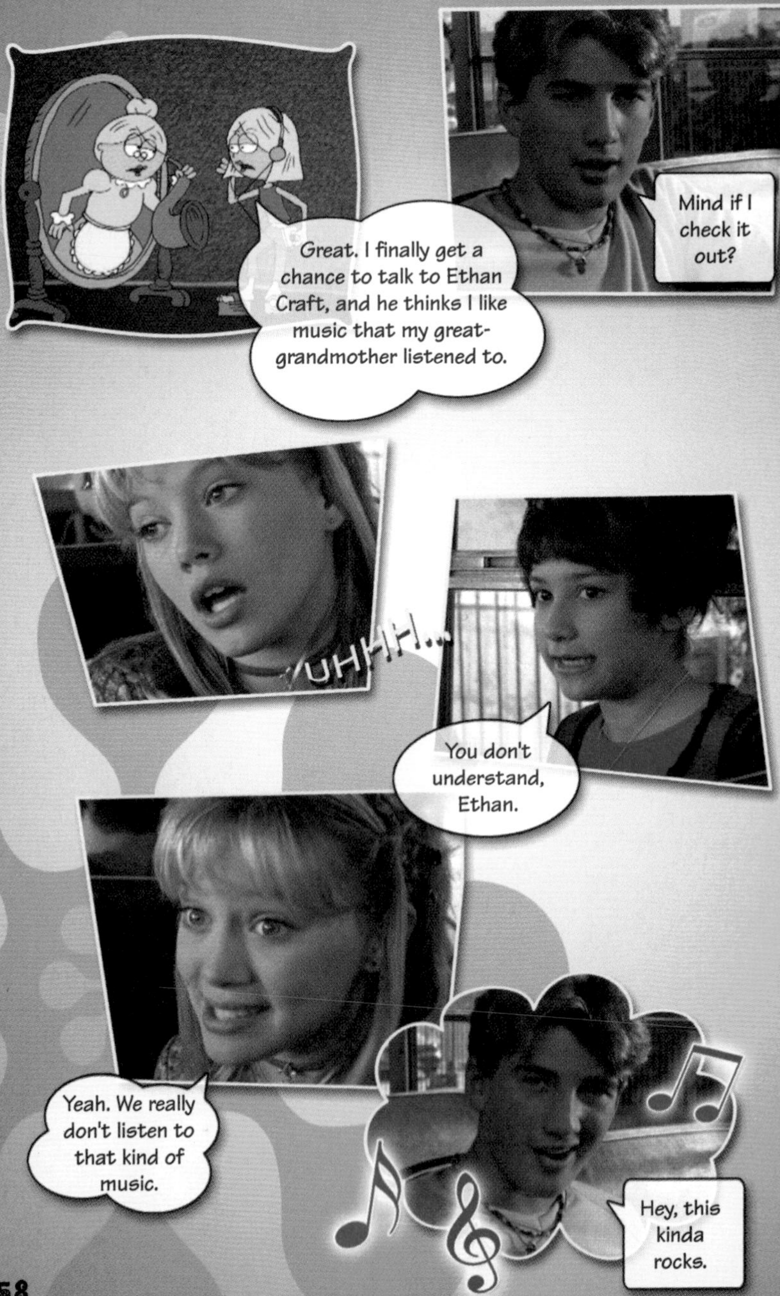
Mind if I check it out?
Great. I finally get a chance to talk to Ethan Craft, and he thinks I like music that my great-grandmother listened to.
UHHH...
You don't understand, Ethan.
Yeah. We really don't listen to that kind of music.
Hey, this kinda rocks.

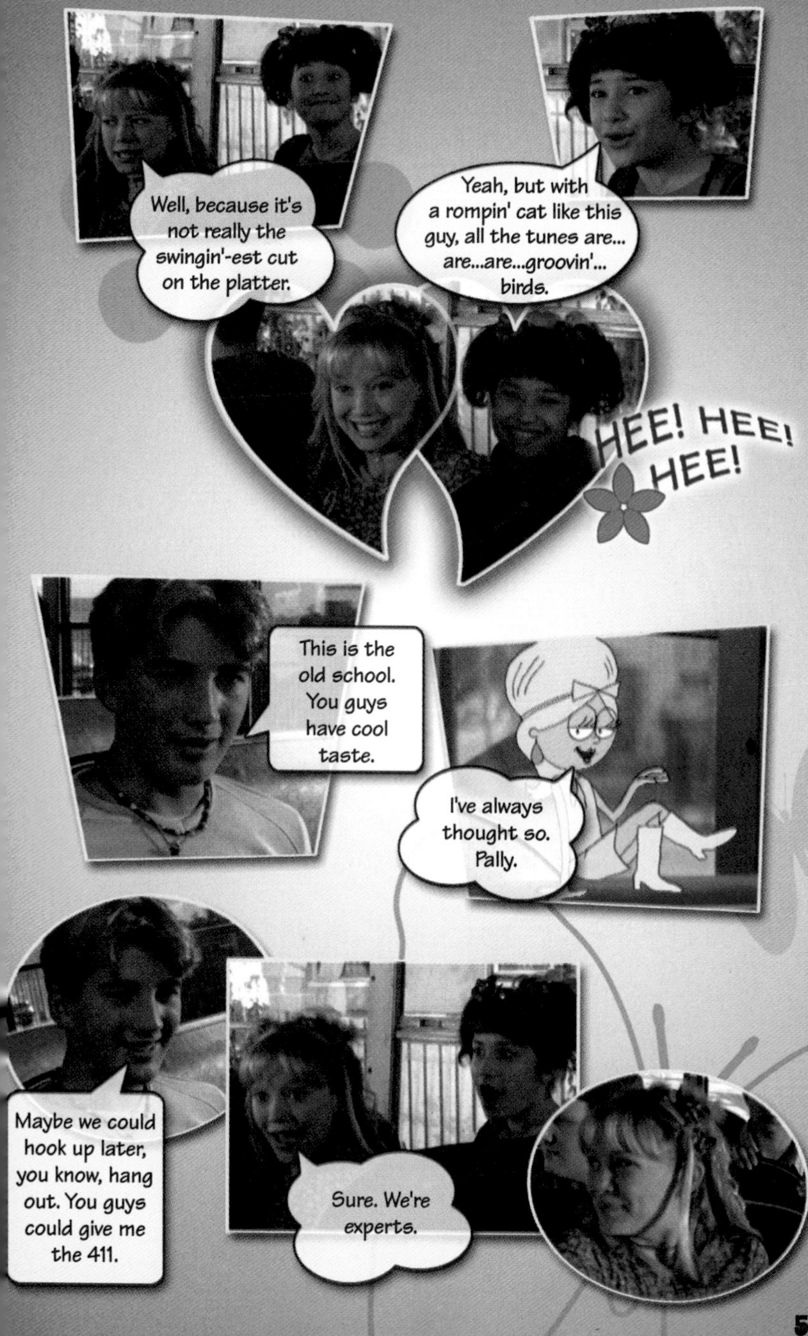

Well, because it's not really the swingin'-est cut on the platter.
Yeah, but with a rompin' cat like this guy, all the tunes are... are...are...groovin'... birds.
HEE! HEE! HEE!
This is the old school. You guys have cool taste.
I've always thought so. Pally.
Maybe we could hook up later, you know, hang out. You guys could give me the 411.
Sure. We're experts.

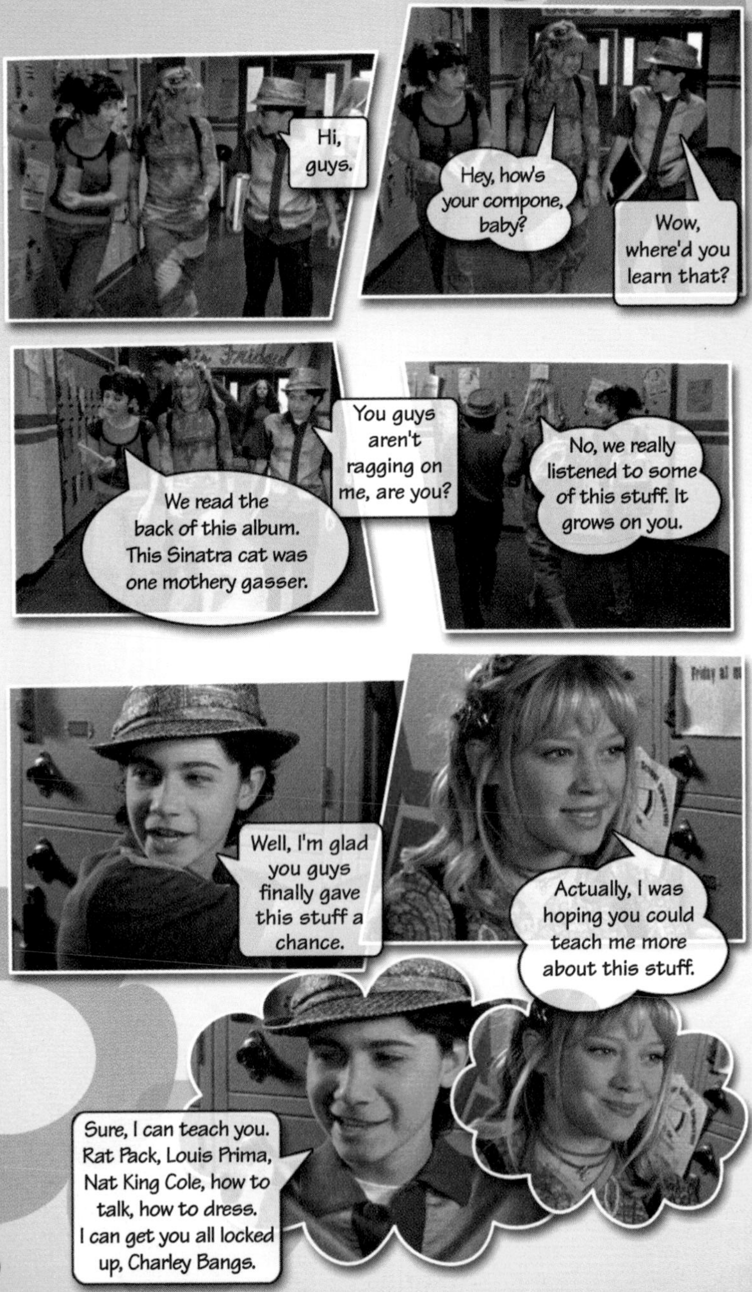
Hi, guys.
Hey, how's your compone, baby?
Wow, where'd you learn that?
You guys aren't ragging on me, are you?
We read the back of this album. This Sinatra cat was one mothery gasser.
No, we really listened to some of this stuff. It grows on you.
Well, I'm glad you guys finally gave this stuff a chance.
Actually, I was hoping you could teach me more about this stuff.
Sure, I can teach you. Rat Pack, Louis Prima, Nat King Cole, how to talk, how to dress. I can get you all locked up, Charley Bangs.

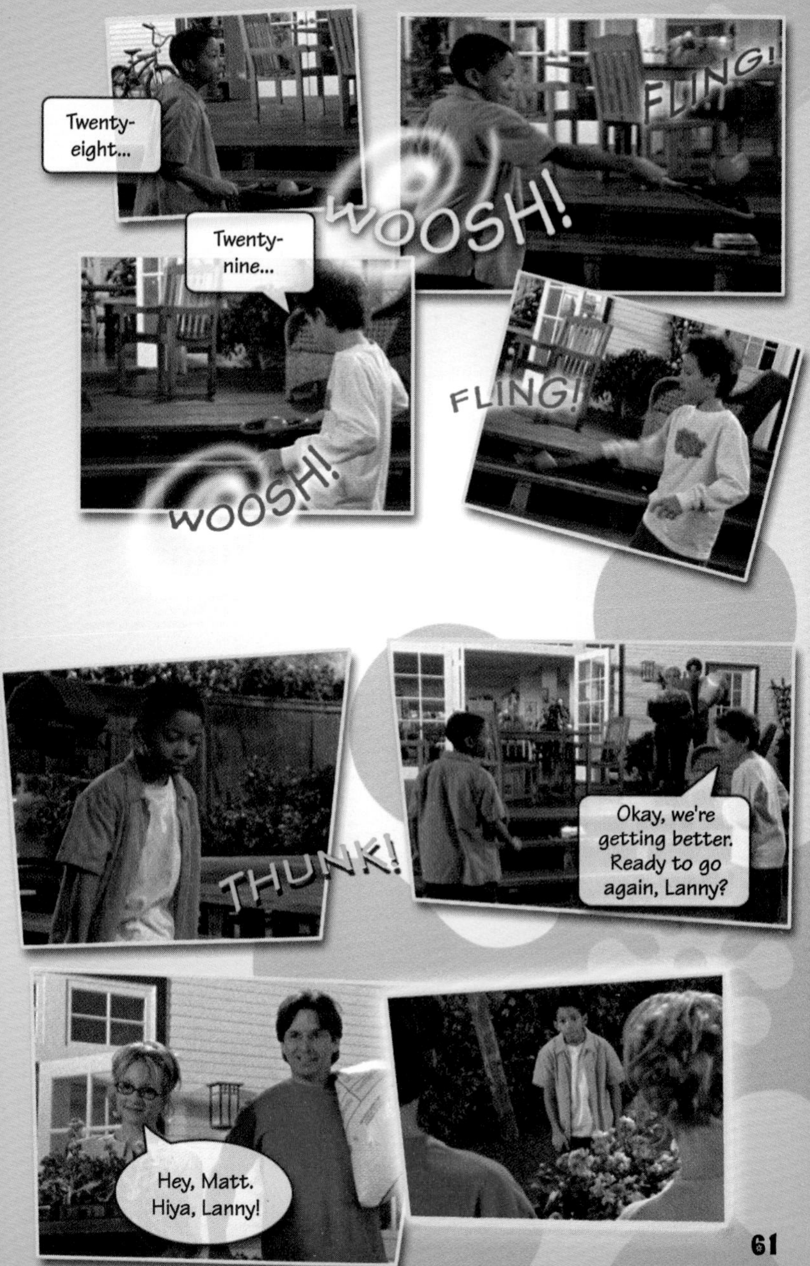
Twenty-
eight...
FLING!
WOOSH!
Twenty-
nine...
FLING!
WOOSH!
THUNK!
Okay, we're getting better. Ready to go again, Lanny?
Hey, Matt. Hiya, Lanny!

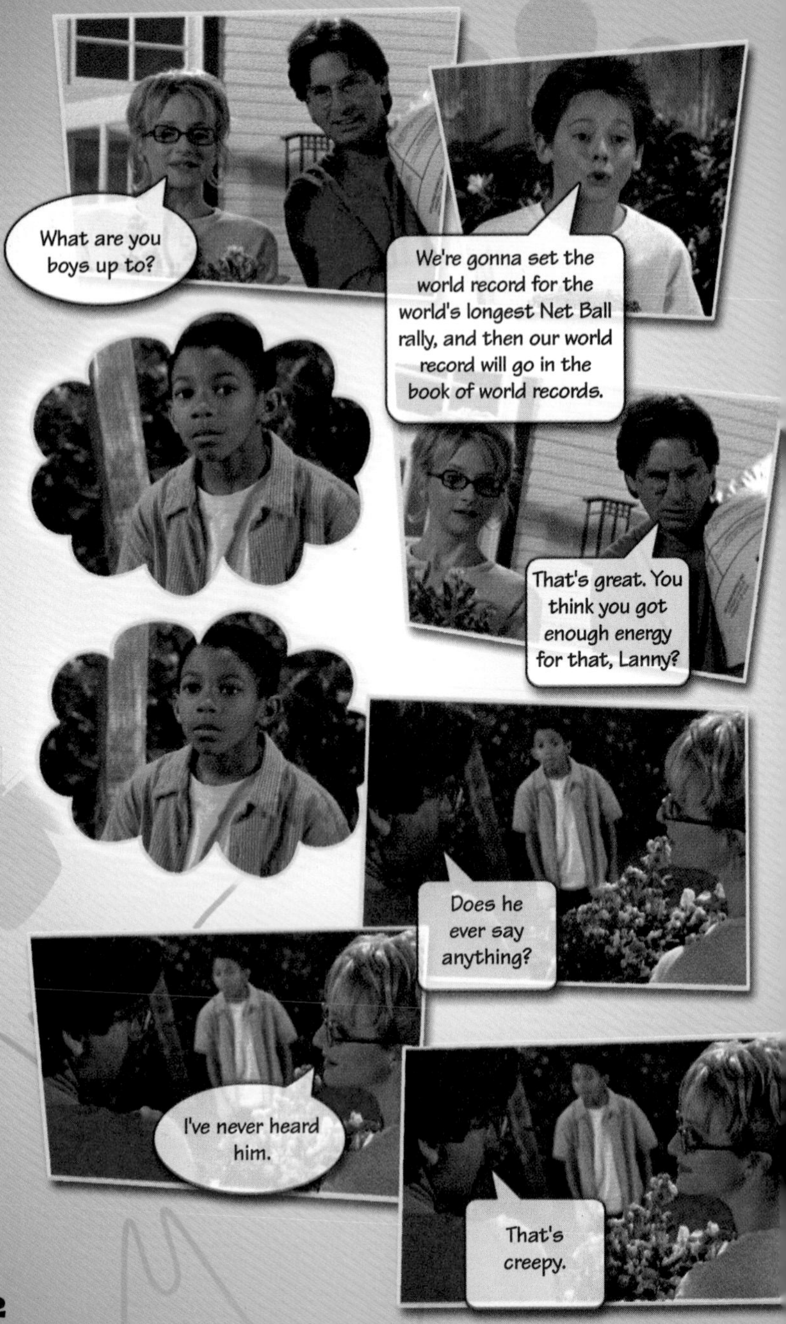

What are you boys up to?
We're gonna set the world record for the world's longest Net Ball rally, and then our world record will go in the book of world records.
That's great. You think you got enough energy for that, Lanny?
Does he ever say anything?
I've never heard him.
That's creepy.

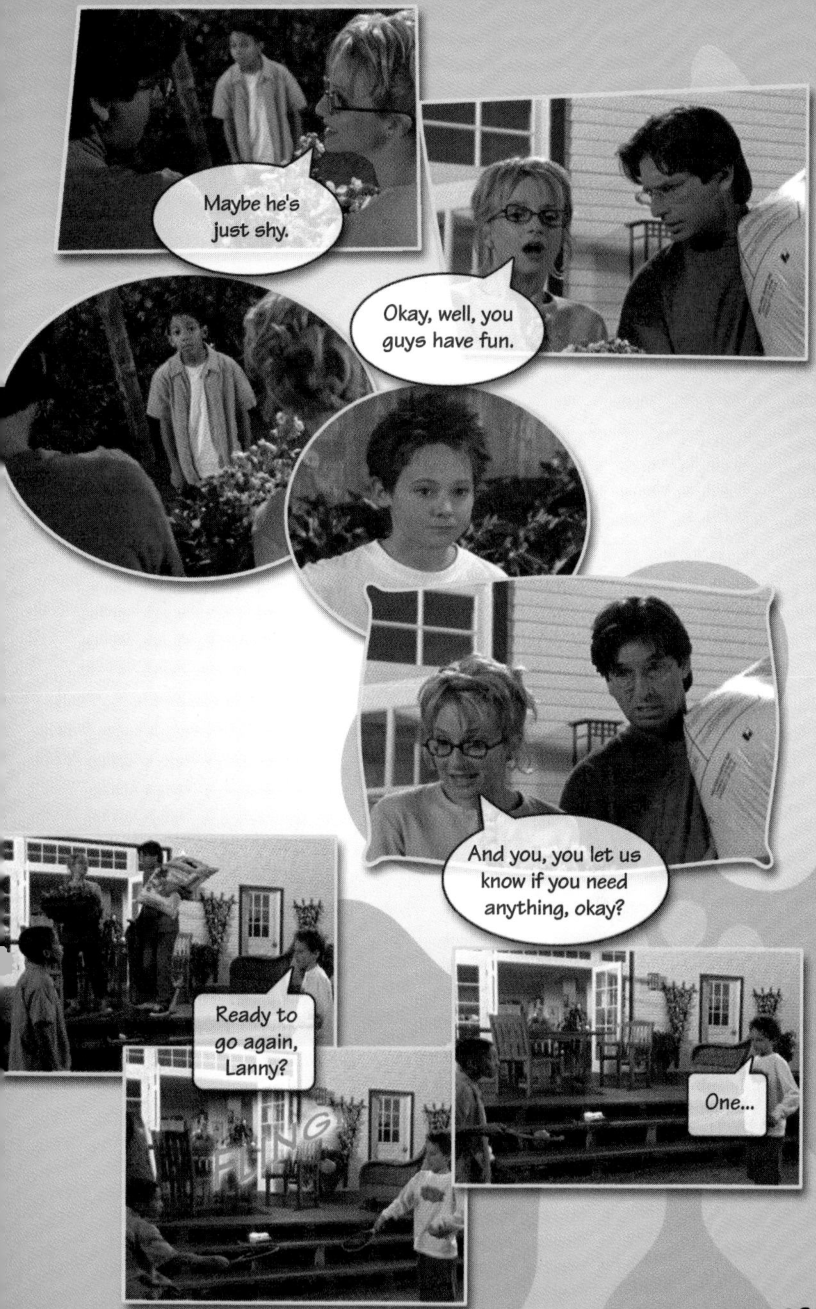
Maybe he's just shy.
Okay, well, you guys have fun.
And you, you let us know if you need anything, okay?
Ready to go again, Lanny?
FLING
One...

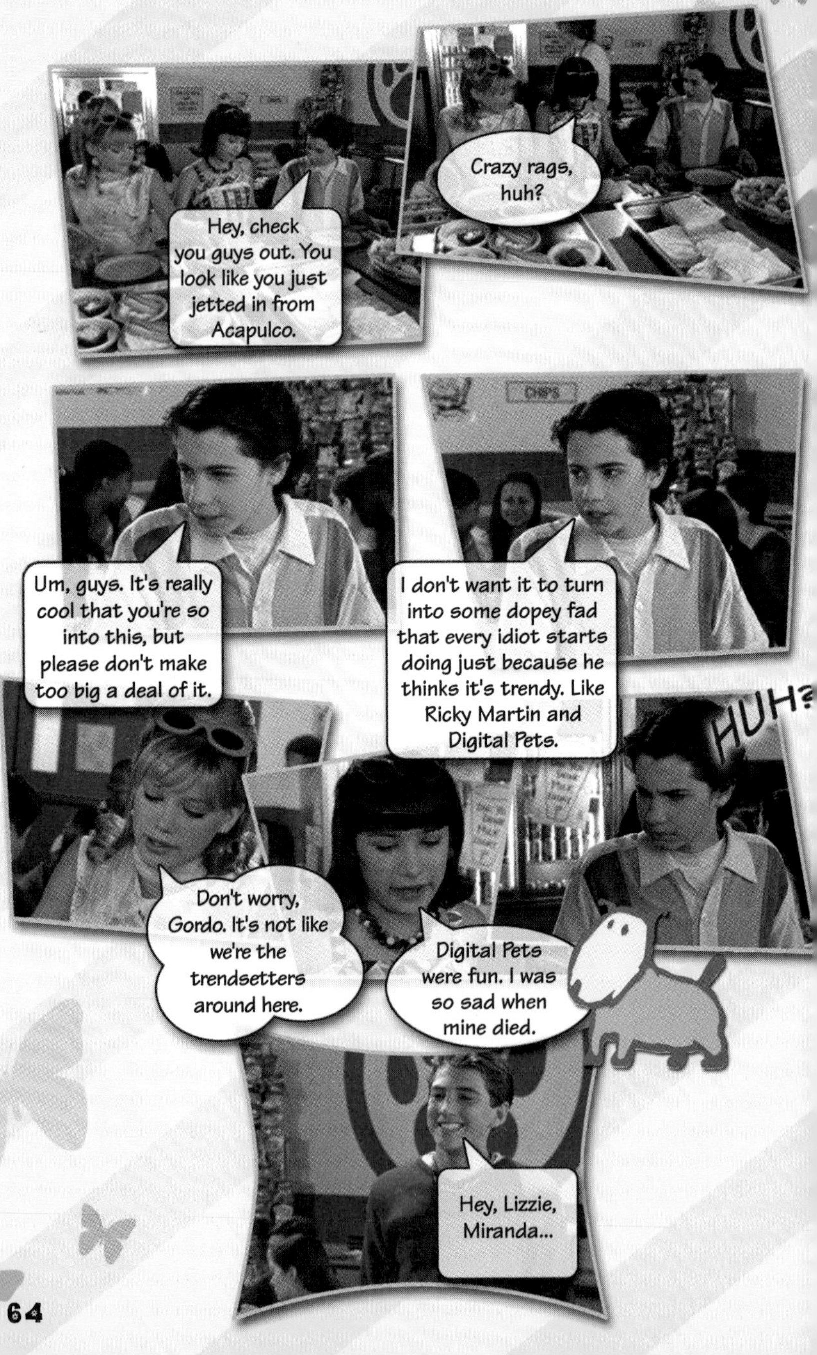
Hey, check you guys out. You look like you just jetted in from Acapulco.
Crazy rags, huh?
Um, guys. It's really cool that you're so into this, but please don't make too big a deal of it.
I don't want it to turn into some dopey fad that every idiot starts doing just because he thinks it's trendy. Like Ricky Martin and Digital Pets.
HUH?
Don't worry, Gordo. It's not like we're the trendsetters around here.
Digital Pets were fun. I was so sad when mine died.
Hey, Lizzie, Miranda...

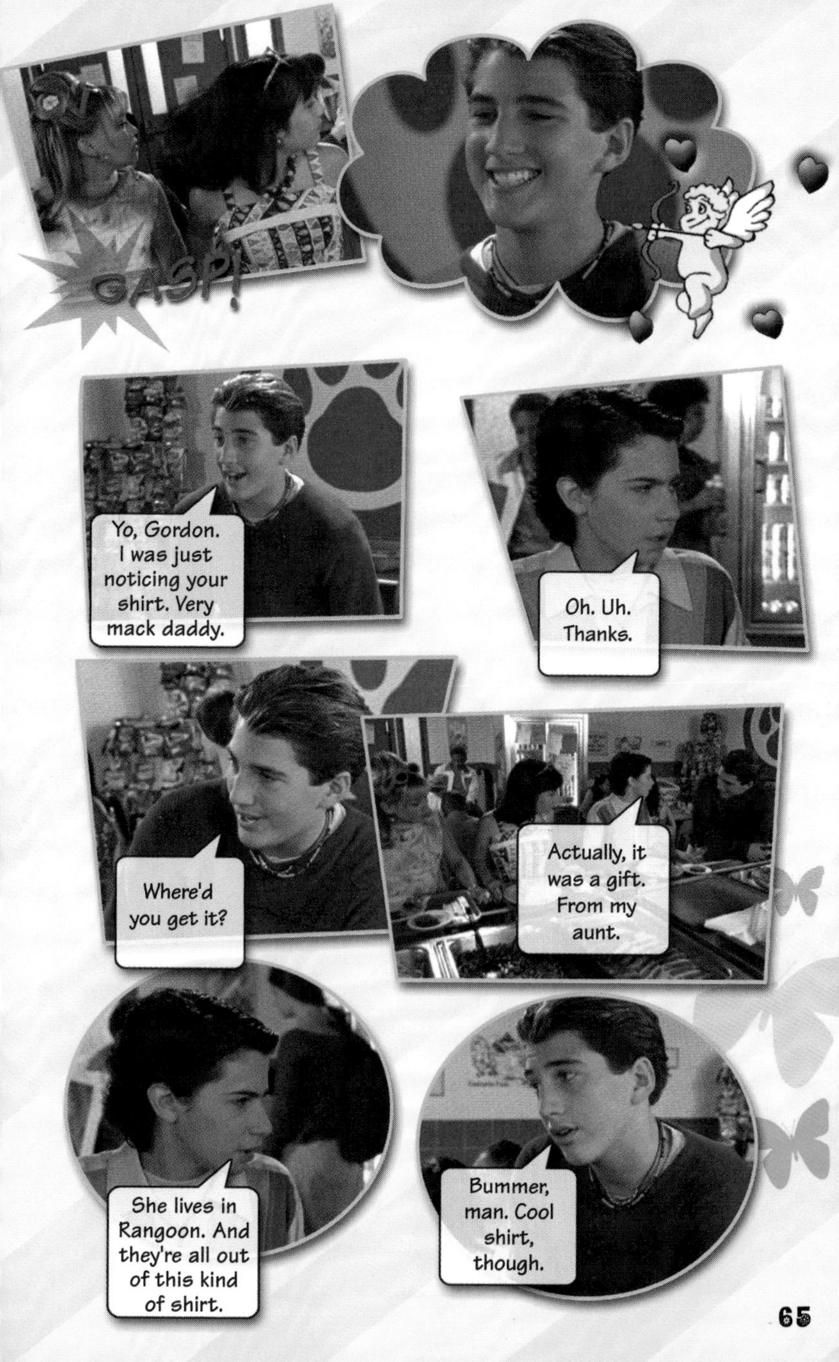

GASP!
Yo, Gordon. I was just noticing your shirt. Very mack daddy.
Oh. Uh. Thanks.
Where'd you get it?
Actually, it was a gift. From my aunt.
She lives in Rangoon. And they're all out of this kind of shirt.
Bummer, man. Cool shirt, though.

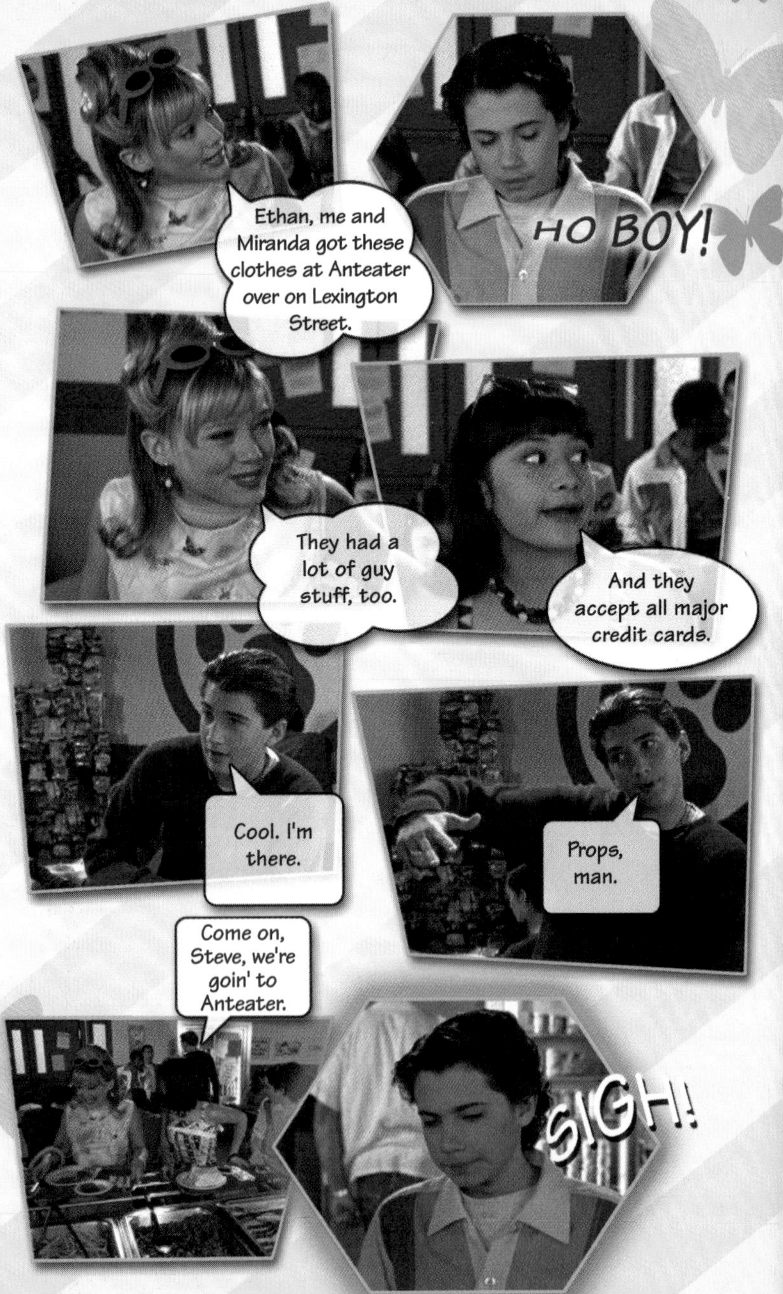
Ethan, me and Miranda got these clothes at Anteater over on Lexington Street.
HO BOY!
They had a lot of guy stuff, too.
And they accept all major credit cards.
Cool. I'm there.
Props, man.
Come on, Steve, we're goin' to Anteater.
SIGH!

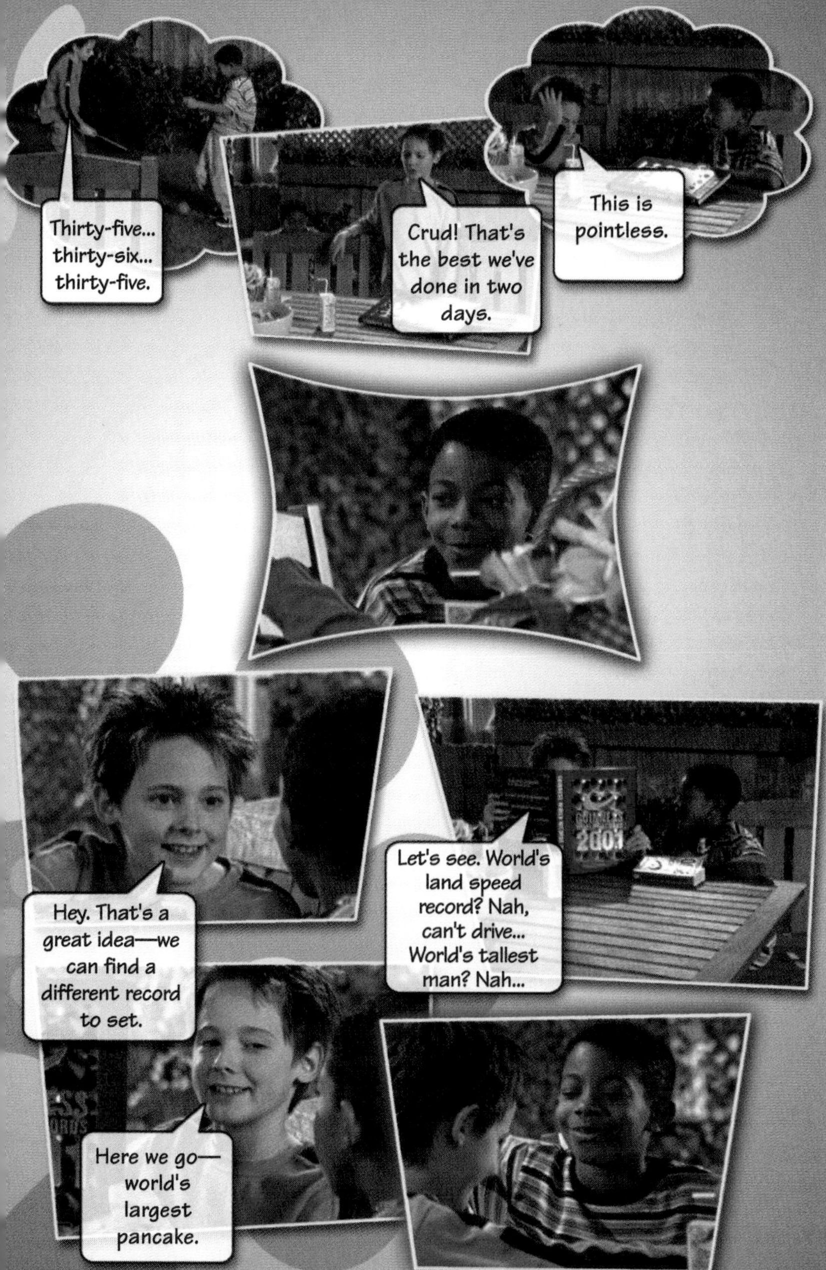
Thirty-five... thirty-six... thirty-five.
Crud! That's the best we've done in two days.
This is pointless.
Hey. That's a great idea—we can find a different record to set.
Let's see. World's land speed record? Nah, can't drive... World's tallest man? Nah...
Here we go—world's largest pancake.

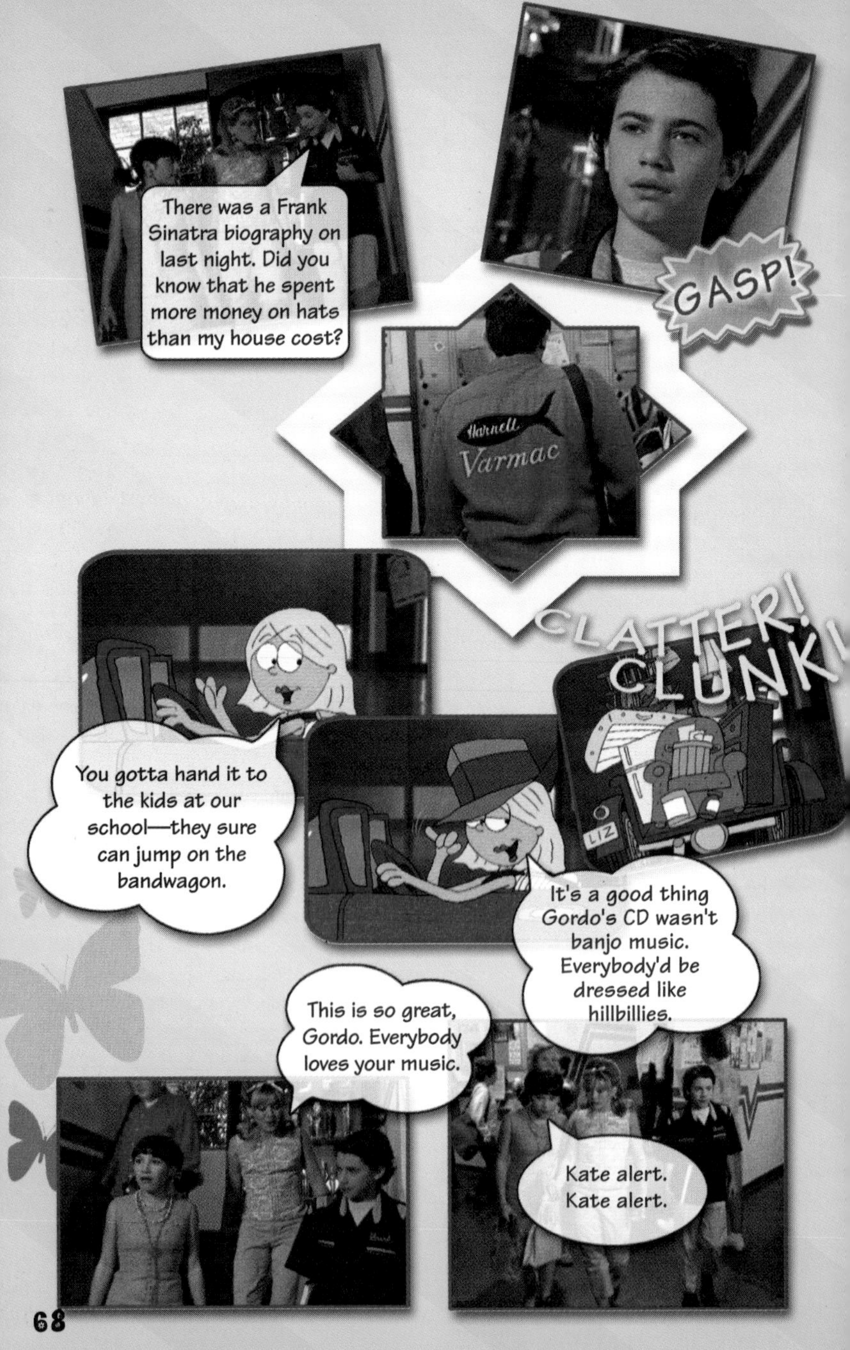
There was a Frank Sinatra biography on last night. Did you know that he spent more money on hats than my house cost?
GASP!
Harnell
Varmac
CLATTER! CLUNK!
LIZ
You gotta hand it to the kids at our school—they sure can jump on the bandwagon.
It's a good thing Gordo's CD wasn't banjo music. Everybody'd be dressed like hillbillies.
This is so great, Gordo. Everybody loves your music.
Kate alert. Kate alert.

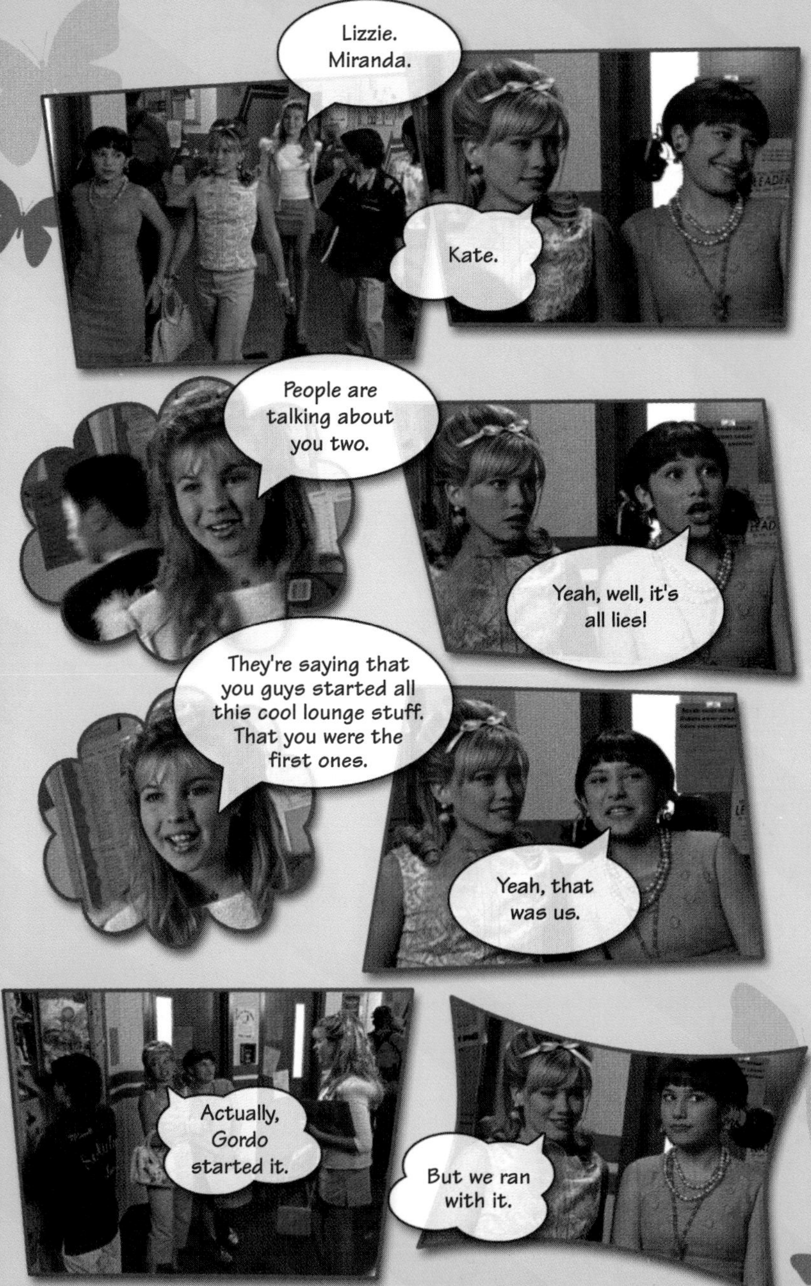

Lizzie. Miranda.
Kate.
People are talking about you two.
Yeah, well, it's all lies!
They're saying that you guys started all this cool lounge stuff. That you were the first ones.
Yeah, that was us.
Actually, Gordo started it.
But we ran with it.

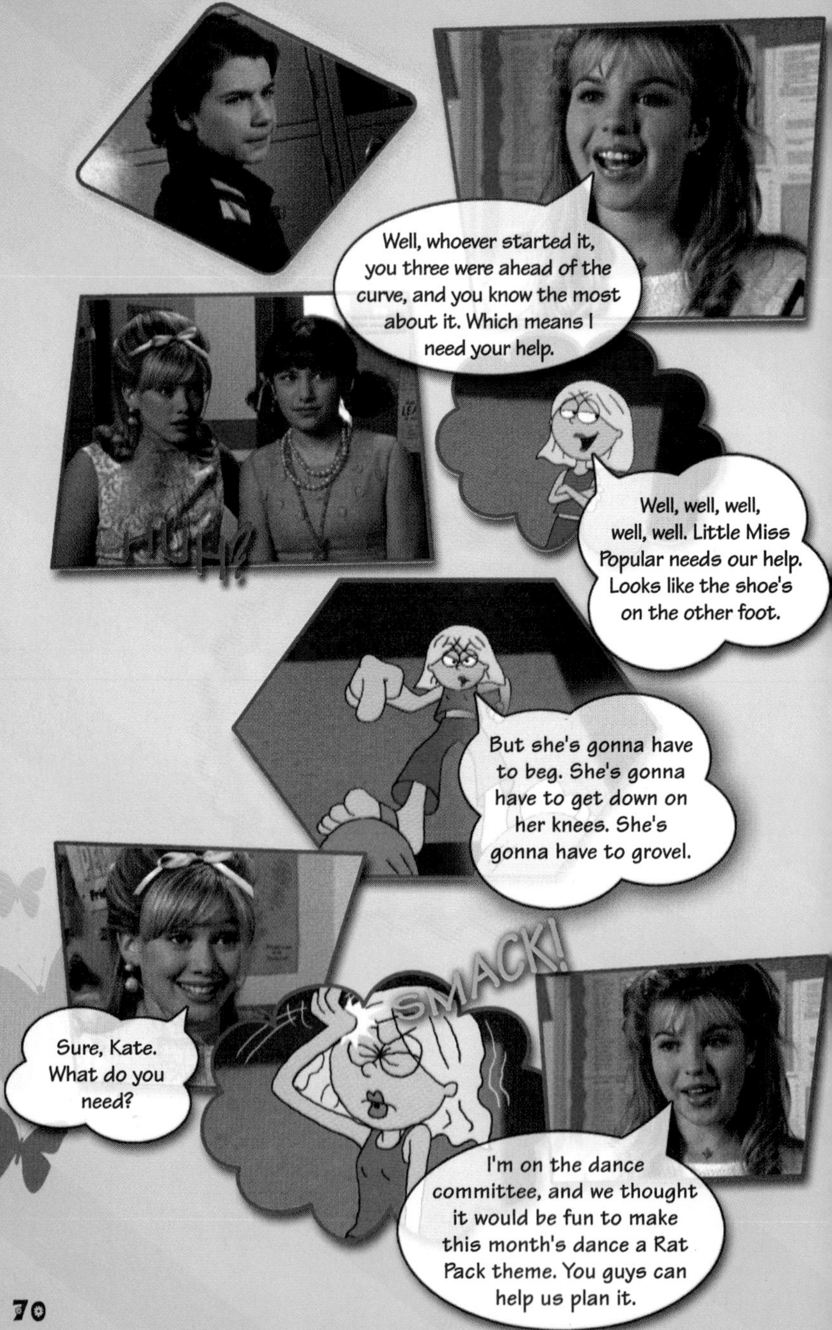
Well, whoever started it, you three were ahead of the curve, and you know the most about it. Which means I need your help.
Well, well, well, well, well. Little Miss Popular needs our help. Looks like the shoe's on the other foot.
But she's gonna have to beg. She's gonna have to get down on her knees. She's gonna have to grovel.
Sure, Kate. What do you need?
SMACK!
I'm on the dance committee, and we thought it would be fun to make this month's dance a Rat Pack theme. You guys can help us plan it.

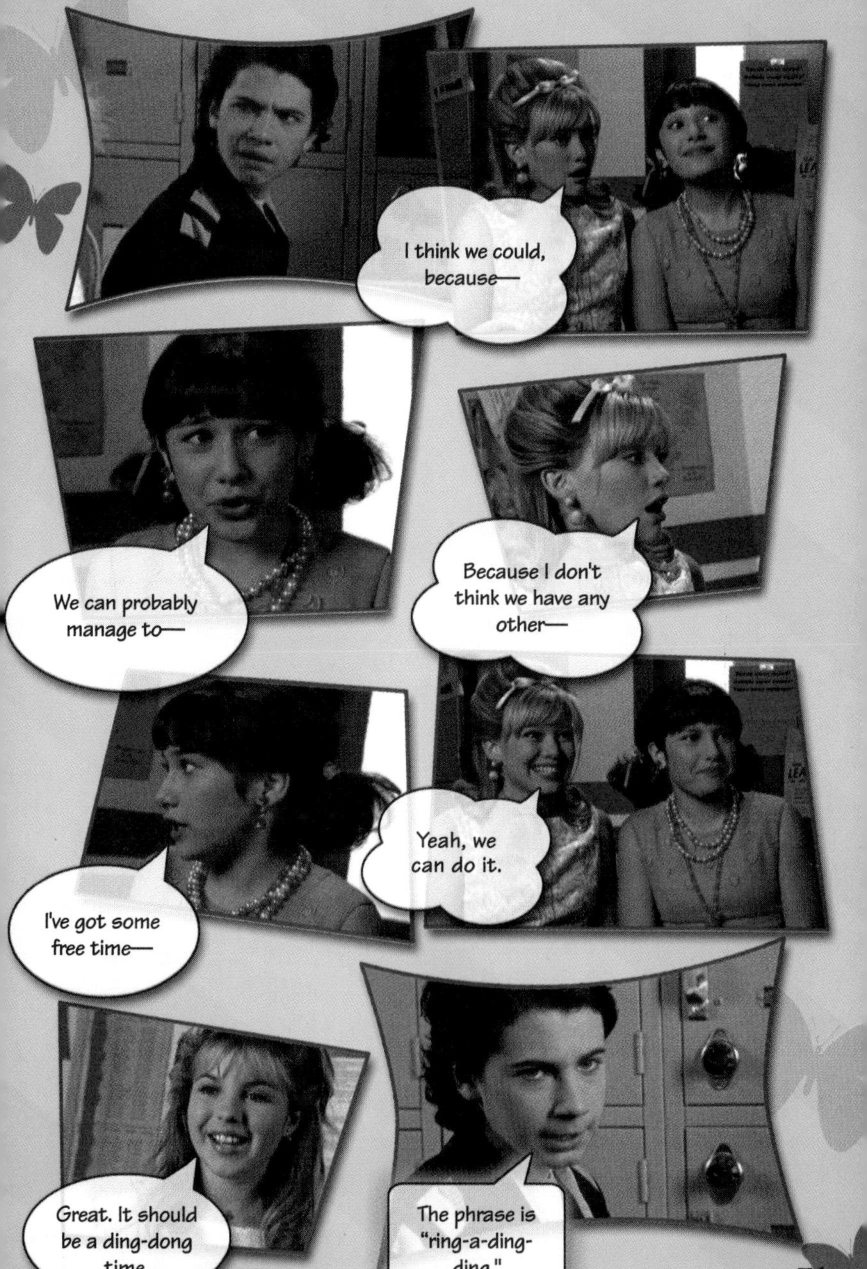
I think we could, because—
We can probably manage to—
Because I don't think we have any other—
I've got some free time—
Yeah, we can do it.
Great. It should be a ding-dong time.
The phrase is "ring-a-ding-ding."

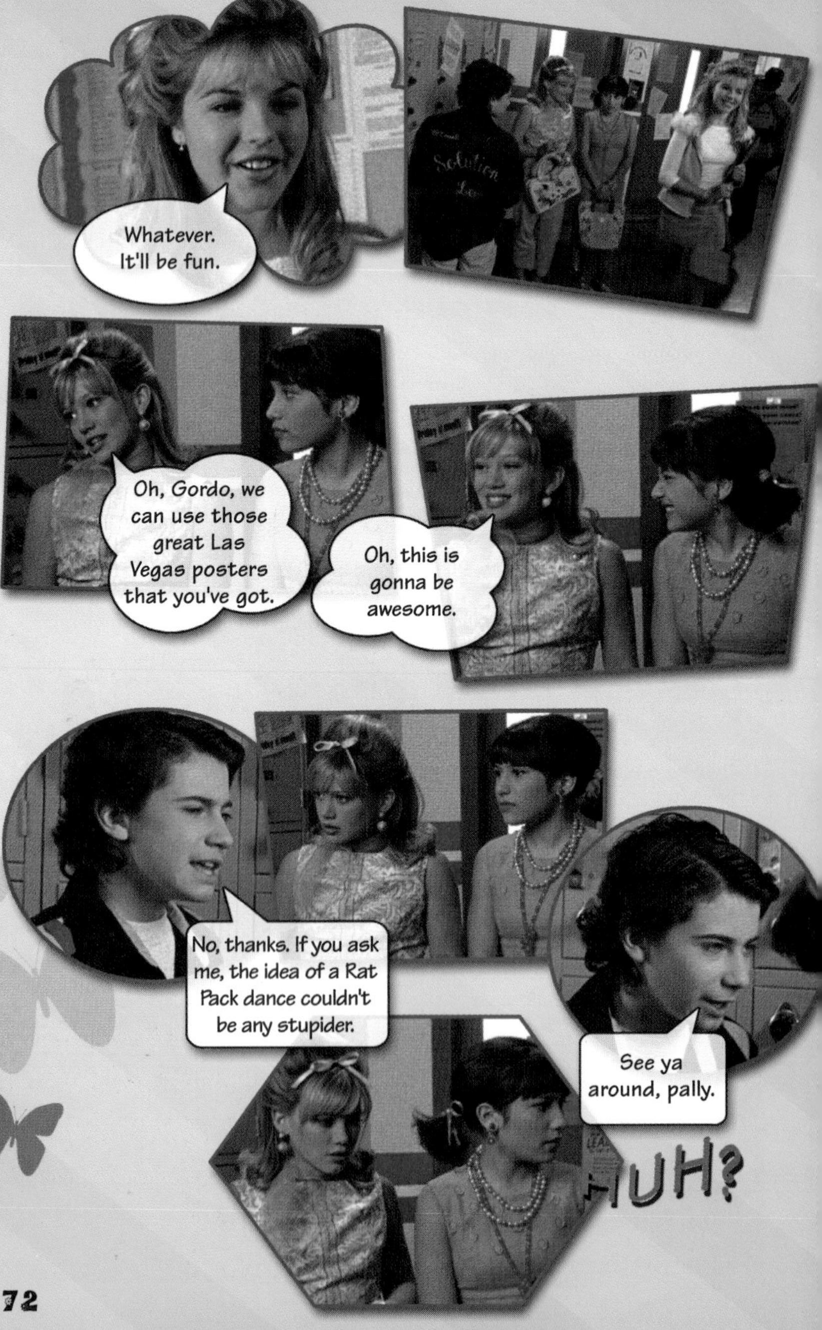

Whatever. It'll be fun.
Oh, Gordo, we can use those great Las Vegas posters that you've got.
Oh, this is gonna be awesome.
No, thanks. If you ask me, the idea of a Rat Pack dance couldn't be any stupider.
See ya around, pally.
HUH?

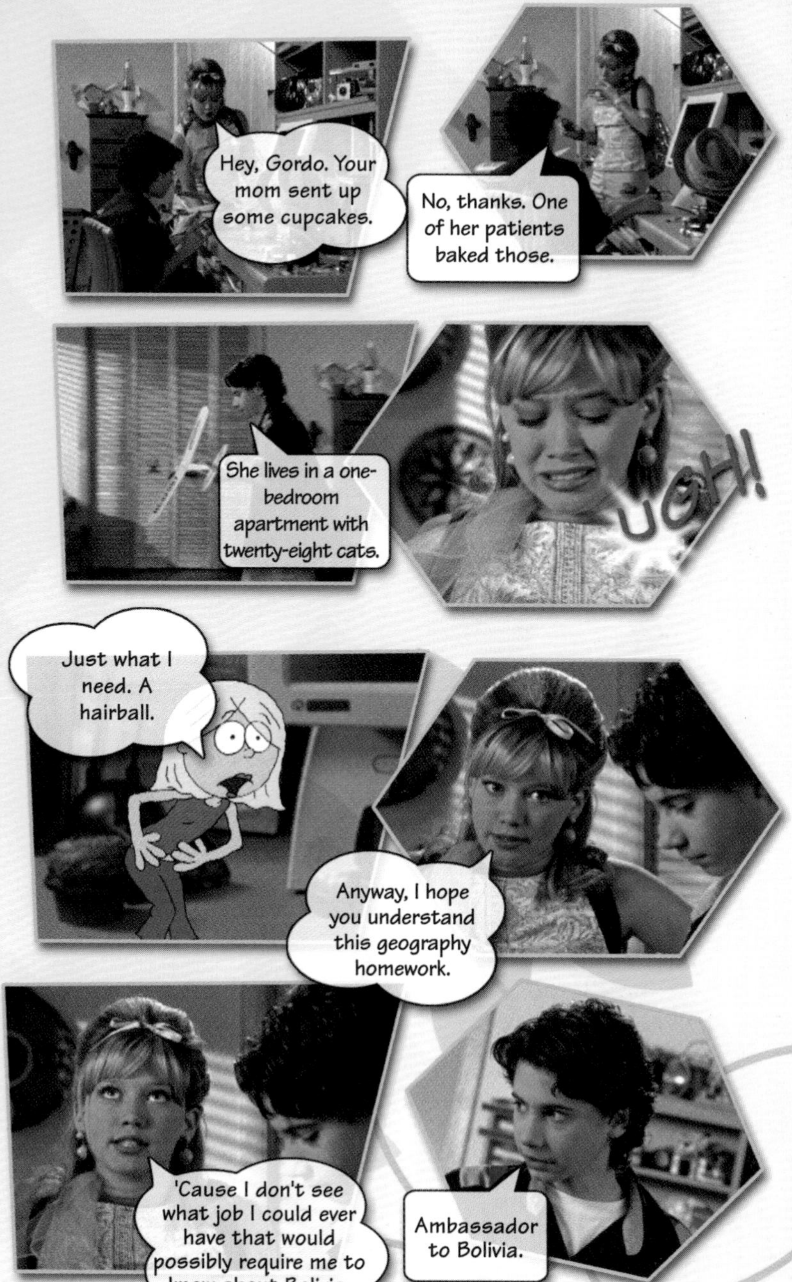

Hey, Gordo. Your mom sent up some cupcakes.
No, thanks. One of her patients baked those.
She lives in a one-bedroom apartment with twenty-eight cats.
UGH!
Just what I need. A hairball.
Anyway, I hope you understand this geography homework.
'Cause I don't see what job I could ever have that would possibly require me to know about Bolivia.
Ambassador to Bolivia.

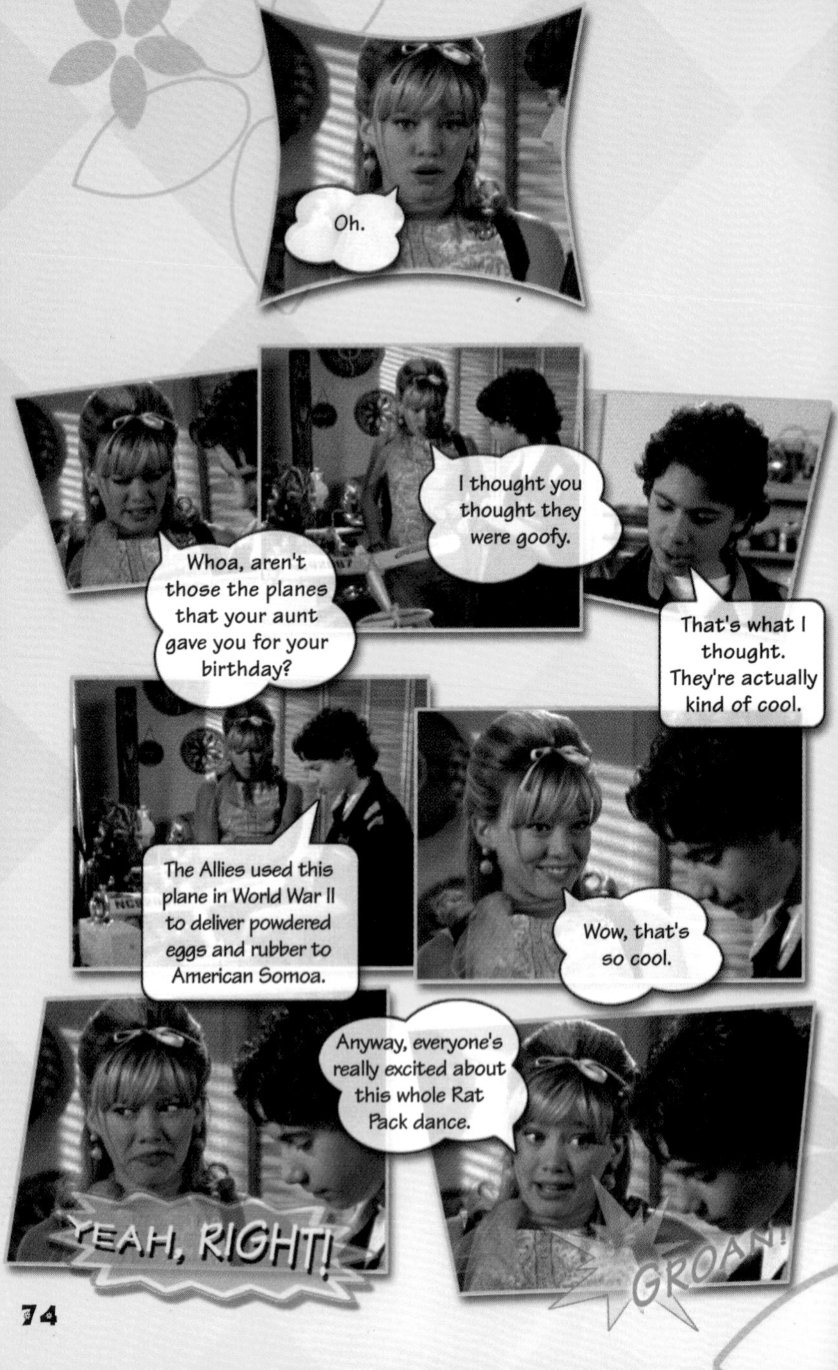
Oh.
Whoa, aren't those the planes that your aunt gave you for your birthday?
I thought you thought they were goofy.
That's what I thought. They're actually kind of cool.
The Allies used this plane in World War II to deliver powdered eggs and rubber to American Somoa.
Wow, that's so cool.
Anyway, everyone's really excited about this whole Rat Pack dance.
YEAH, RIGHT!
GROAN!

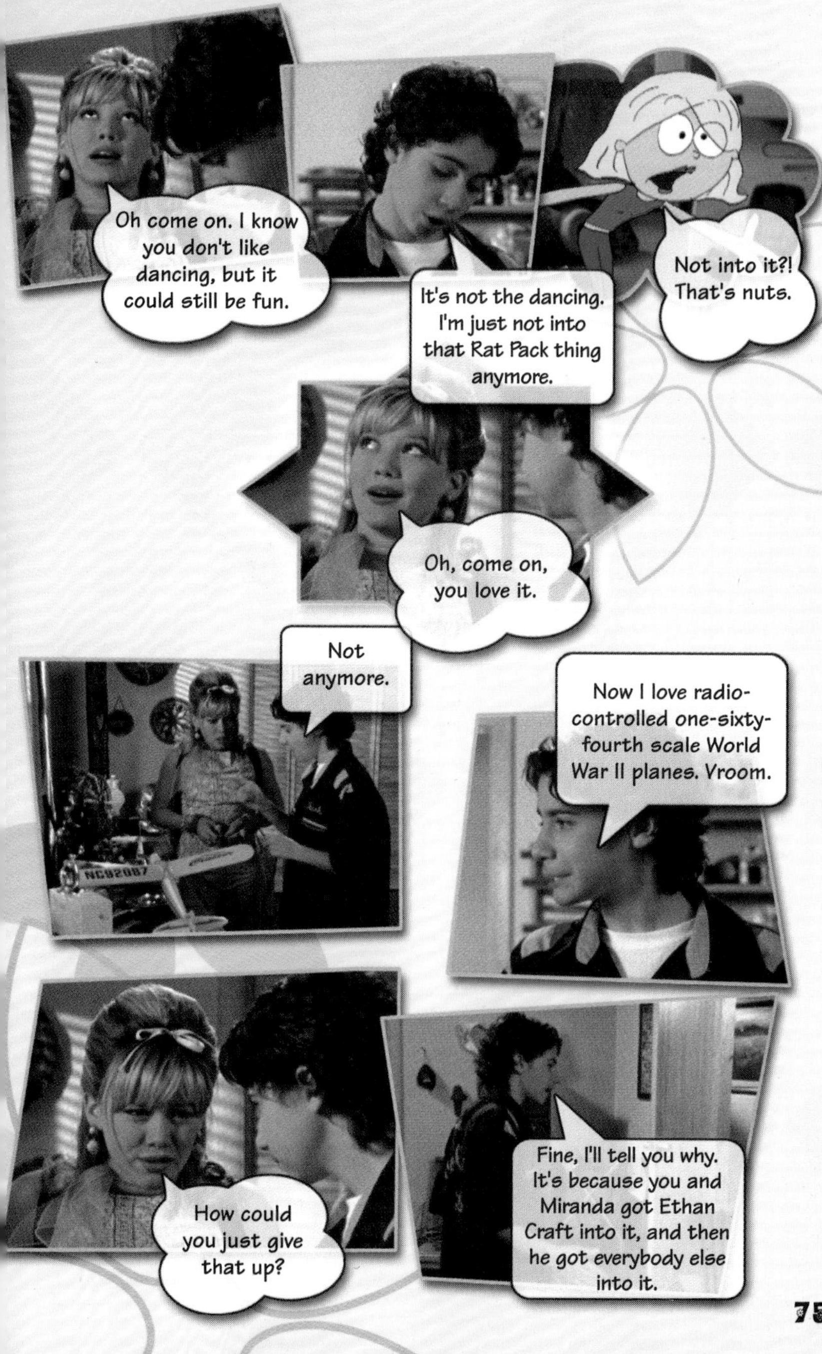

Oh come on. I know you don't like dancing, but it could still be fun.
It's not the dancing. I'm just not into that Rat Pack thing anymore.
Not into it?! That's nuts.
Oh, come on, you love it.
Not anymore.
Now I love radio-controlled one-sixty-fourth scale World War II planes. Vroom.
How could you just give that up?
Fine, I'll tell you why. It's because you and Miranda got Ethan Craft into it, and then he got everybody else into it.

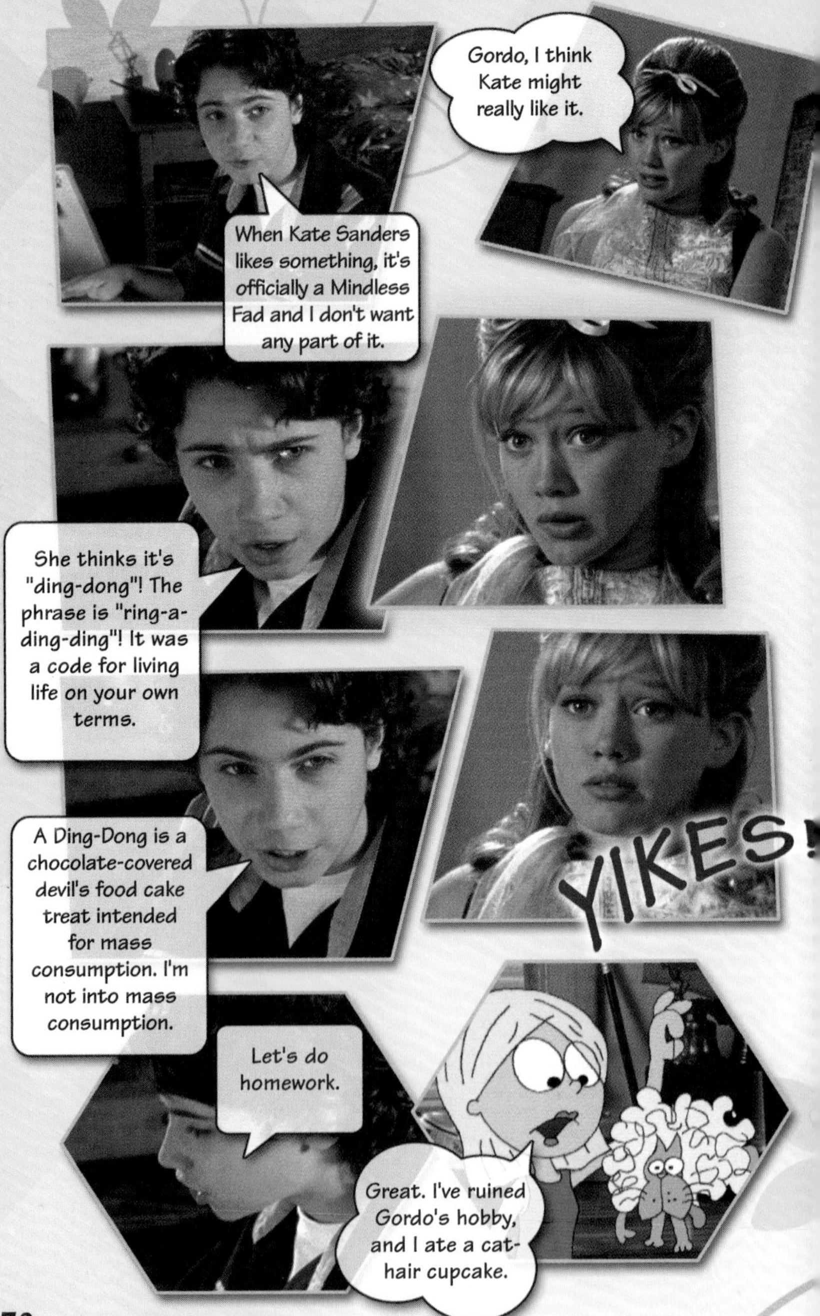

When Kate Sanders likes something, it's officially a Mindless Fad and I don't want any part of it.
Gordo, I think Kate might really like it.
She thinks it's "ding-dong"! The phrase is "ring-a-ding-ding"! It was a code for living life on your own terms.
A Ding-Dong is a chocolate-covered devil's food cake treat intended for mass consumption. I'm not into mass consumption.
YIKES!
Let's do homework.
Great. I've ruined Gordo's hobby, and I ate a cat-hair cupcake.

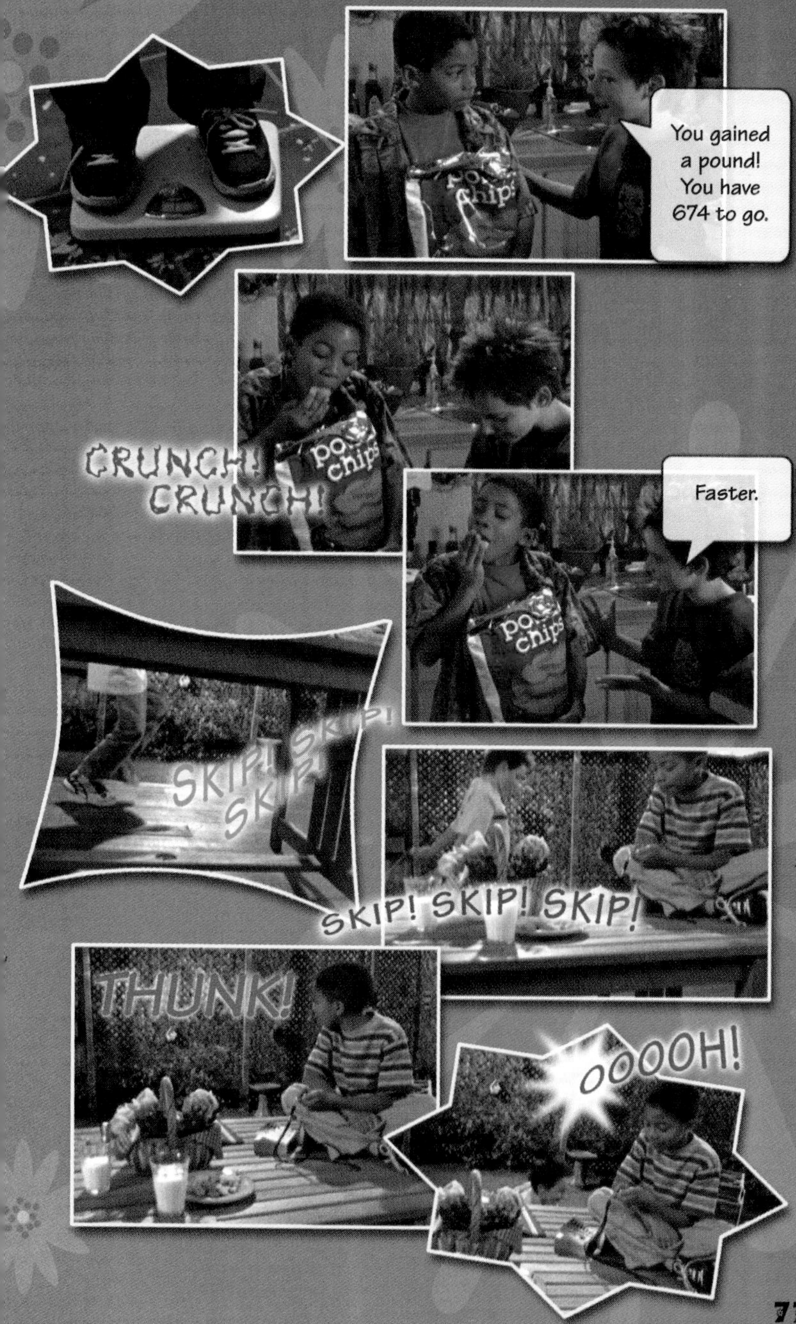
You gained a pound! You have 674 to go.
CRUNCH! CRUNCH!
Faster.
SKIP! SKIP! SKIP!
SKIP! SKIP! SKIP!
THUNK!
OOOOH!

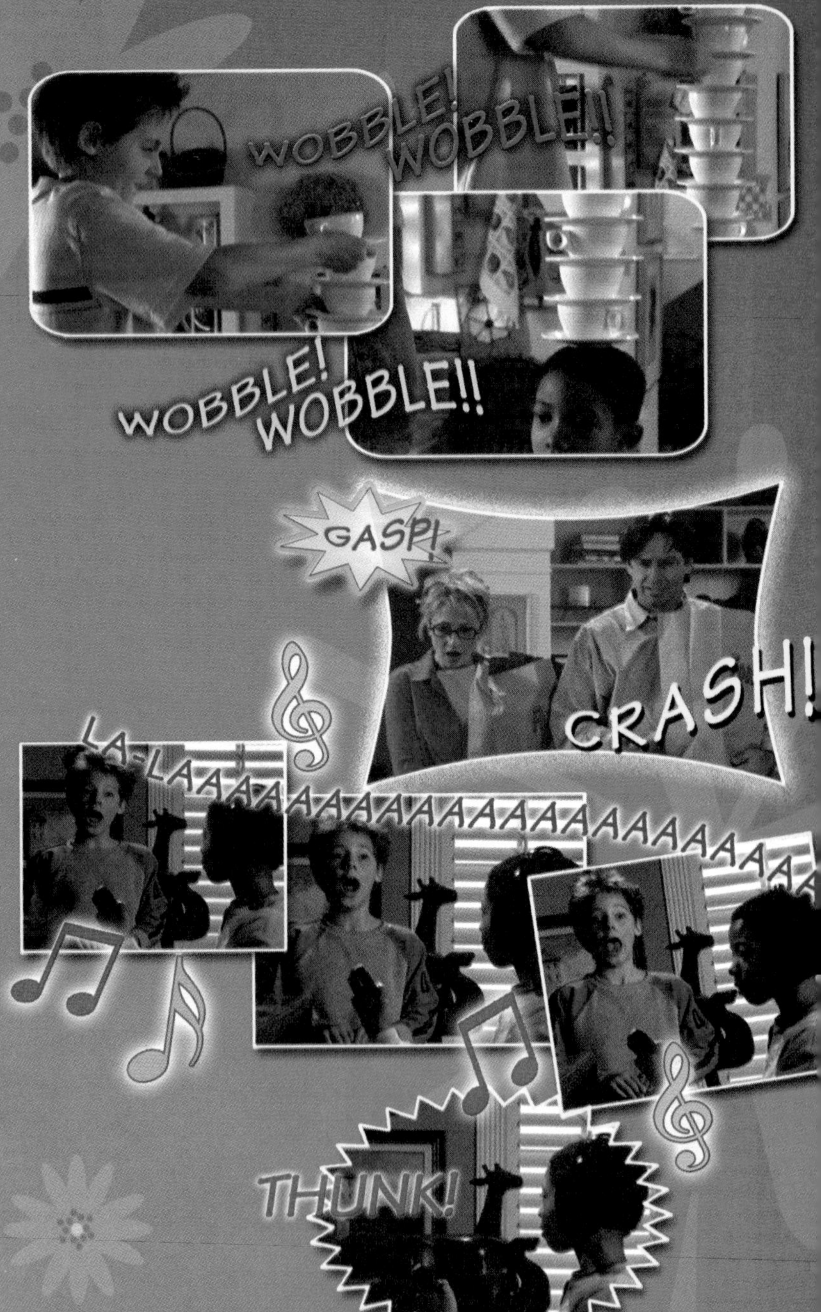
WOBBLE! WOBBLE!!
WOBBLE! WOBBLE!!
GASP!
CRASH!
LA-LAAAAAAAAAAAAAAAAAAAAA
THUNK!

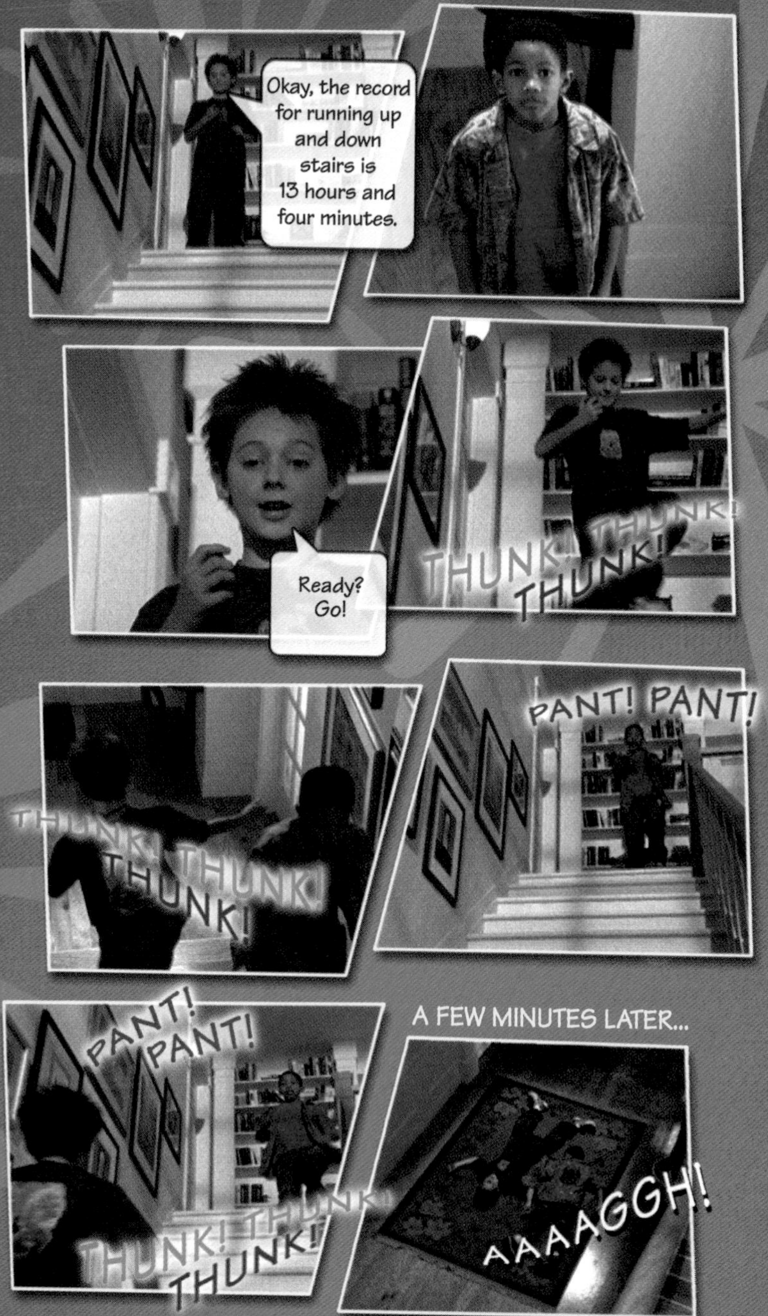
Okay, the record for running up and down stairs is 13 hours and four minutes.
Ready? Go!
THUNK! THUNK! THUNK!
THUNK! THUNK! THUNK!
PANT! PANT!
PANT! PANT!
THUNK! THUNK! THUNK!
A FEW MINUTES LATER...
AAAAGGH!

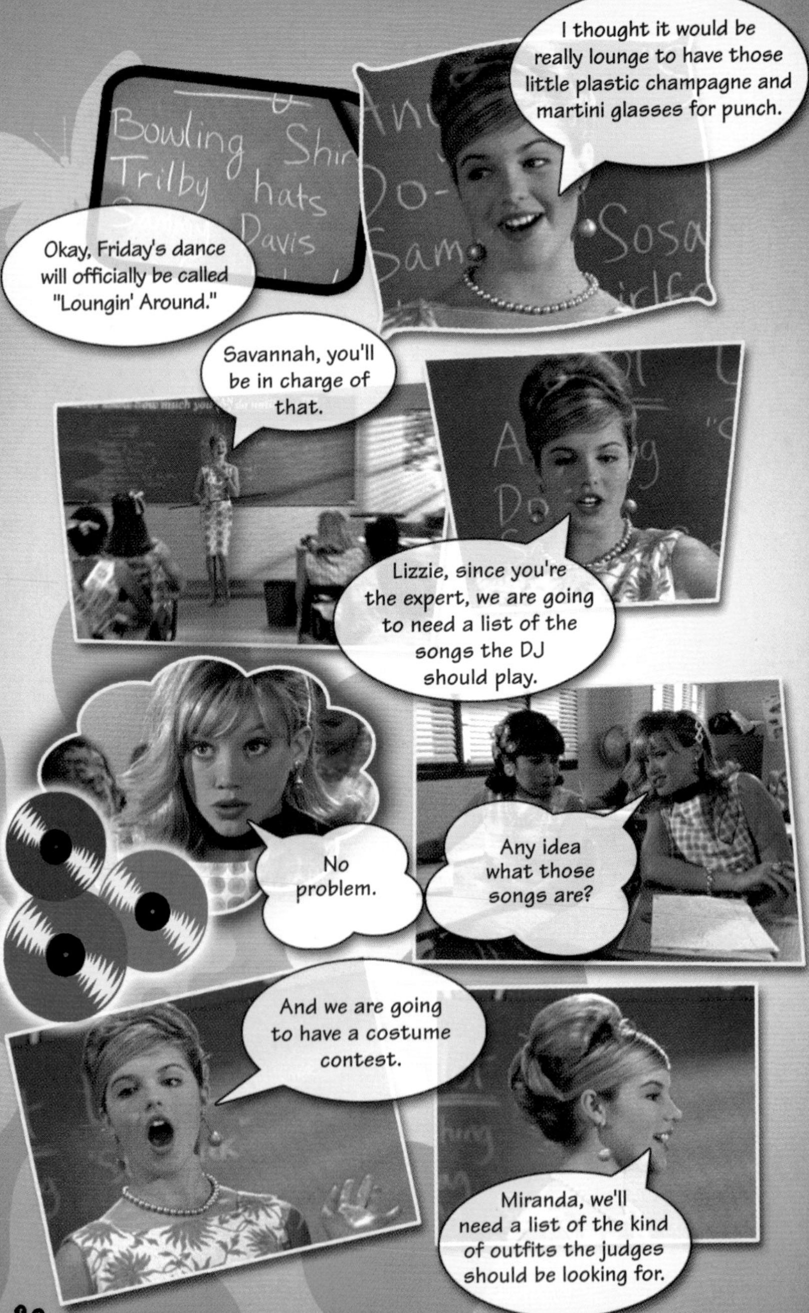
Okay, Friday's dance will officially be called "Loungin' Around."
I thought it would be really lounge to have those little plastic champagne and martini glasses for punch.
Savannah, you'll be in charge of that.
Lizzie, since you're the expert, we are going to need a list of the songs the DJ should play.
No problem.
Any idea what those songs are?
And we are going to have a costume contest.
Miranda, we'll need a list of the kind of outfits the judges should be looking for.

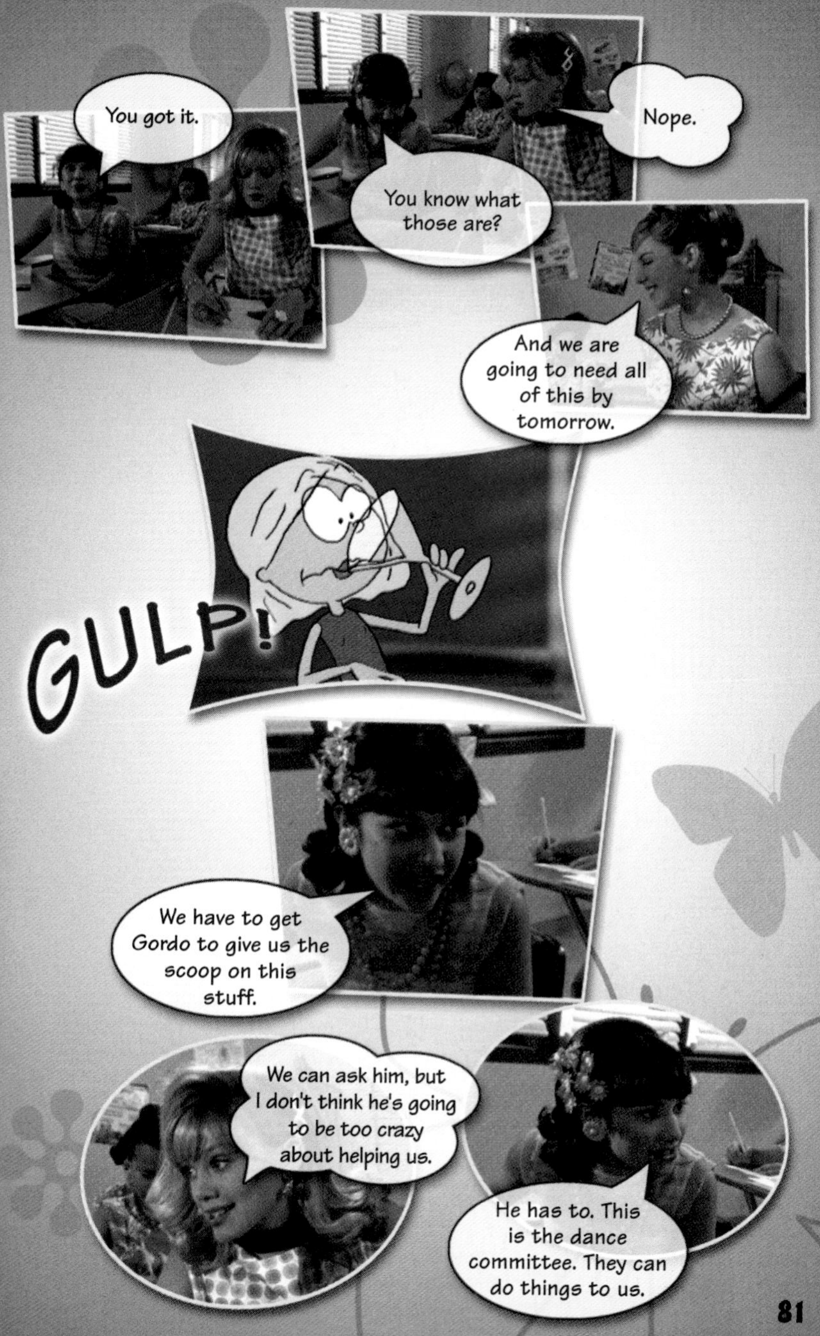

You got it.
You know what those are?
Nope.
And we are going to need all of this by tomorrow.
GULP!
We have to get Gordo to give us the scoop on this stuff.
We can ask him, but I don't think he's going to be too crazy about helping us.
He has to. This is the dance committee. They can do things to us.

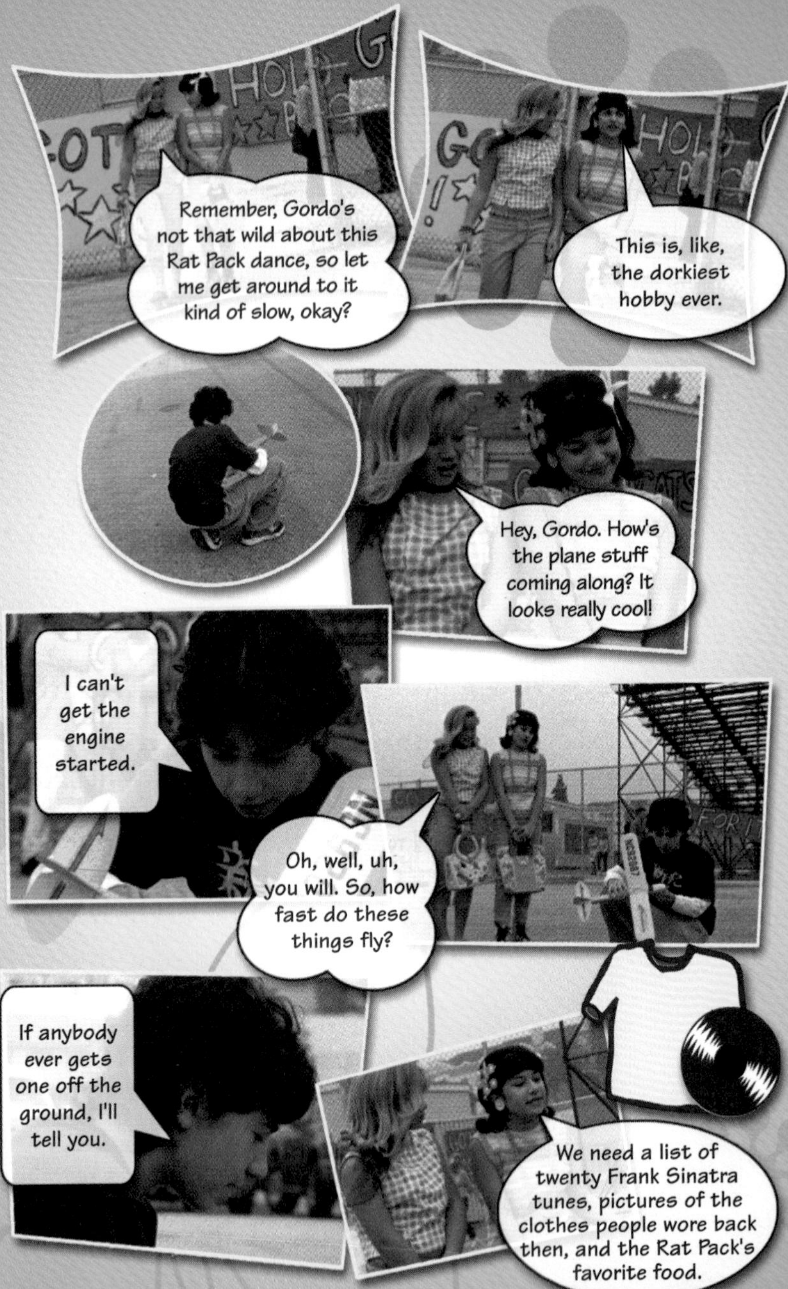
Remember, Gordo's not that wild about this Rat Pack dance, so let me get around to it kind of slow, okay?
This is, like, the dorkiest hobby ever.
Hey, Gordo. How's the plane stuff coming along? It looks really cool!
I can't get the engine started.
Oh, well, uh, you will. So, how fast do these things fly?
If anybody ever gets one off the ground, I'll tell you.
We need a list of twenty Frank Sinatra tunes, pictures of the clothes people wore back then, and the Rat Pack's favorite food.

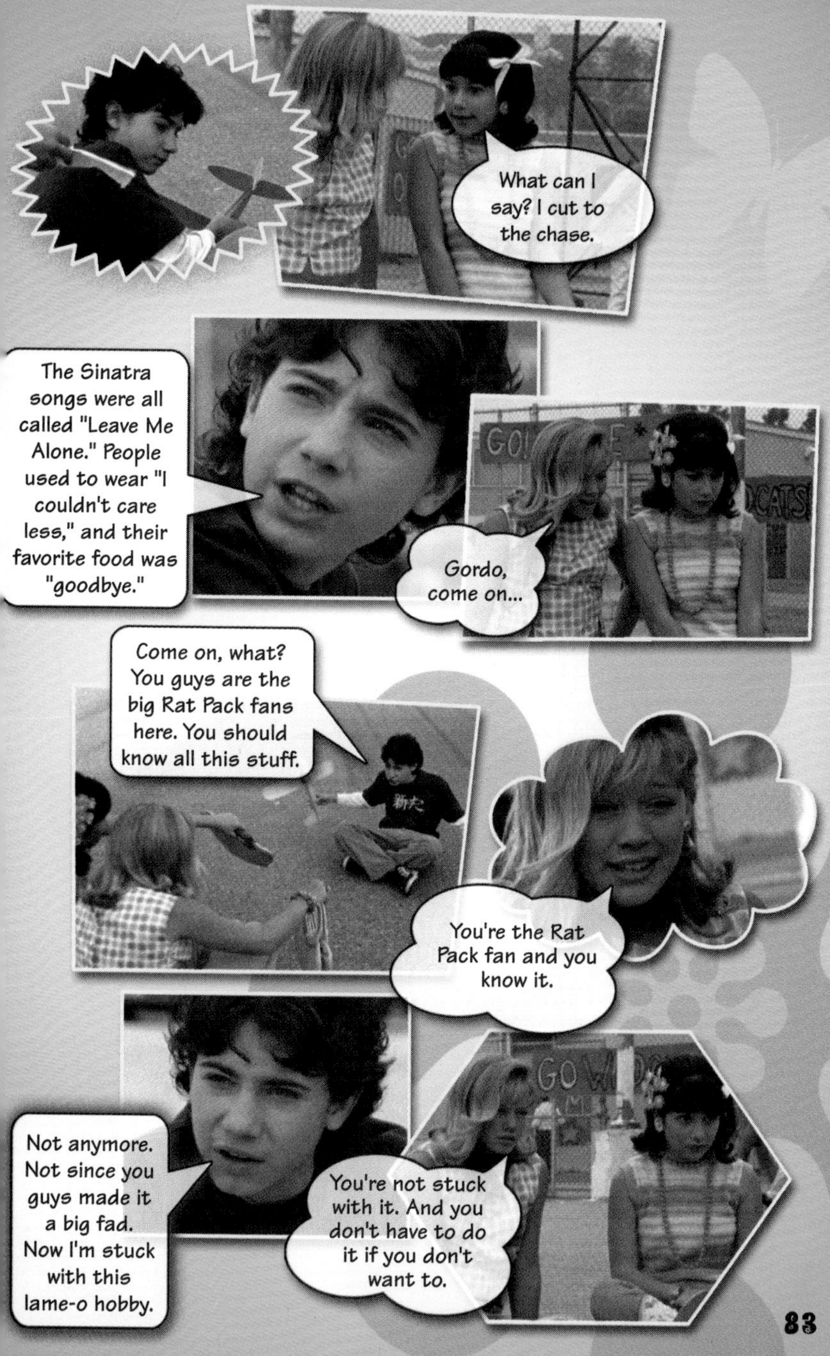
What can I say? I cut to the chase.
The Sinatra songs were all called "Leave Me Alone." People used to wear "I couldn't care less," and their favorite food was "goodbye."
Gordo, come on...
Come on, what? You guys are the big Rat Pack fans here. You should know all this stuff.
You're the Rat Pack fan and you know it.
Not anymore. Not since you guys made it a big fad. Now I'm stuck with this lame-o hobby.
You're not stuck with it. And you don't have to do it if you don't want to.

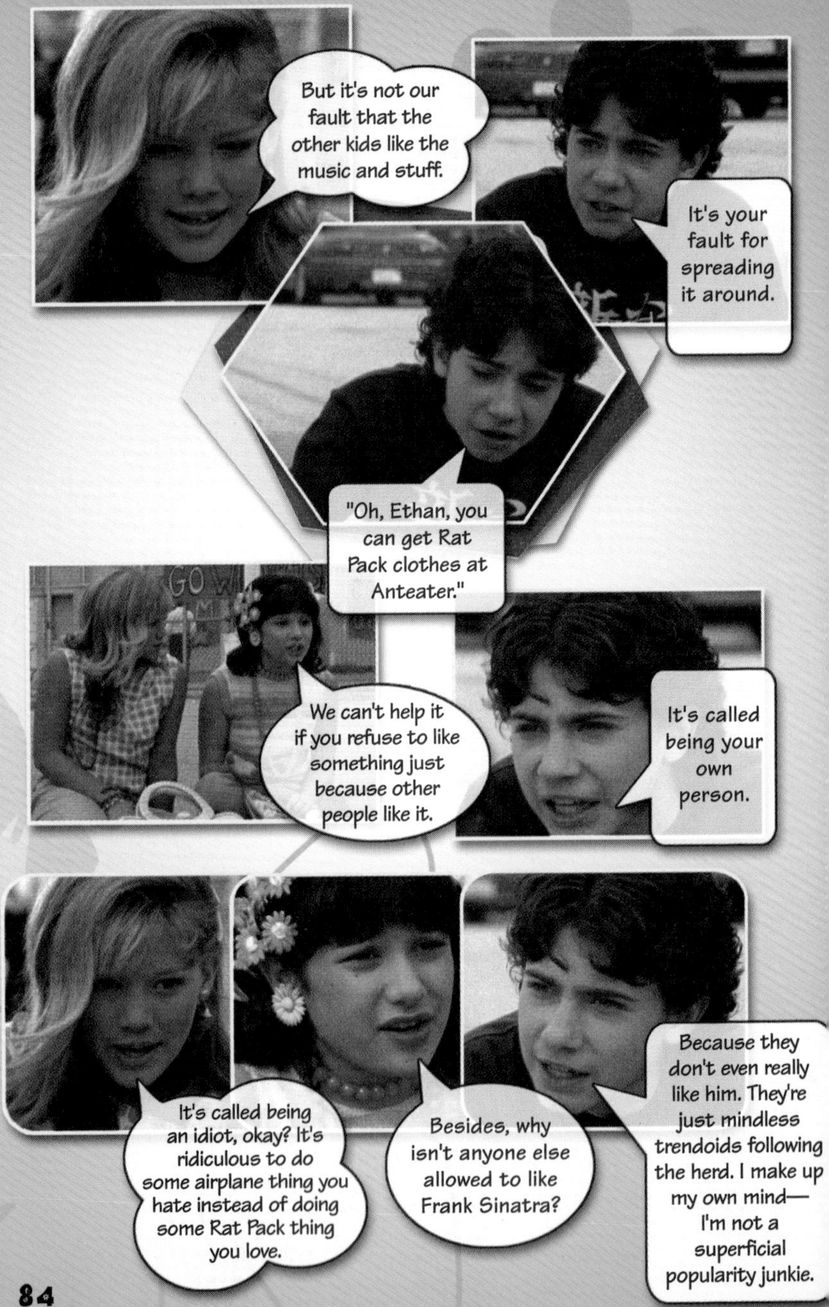

But it's not our fault that the other kids like the music and stuff.
It's your fault for spreading it around.
"Oh, Ethan, you can get Rat Pack clothes at Anteater."
We can't help it if you refuse to like something just because other people like it.
It's called being your own person.
It's called being an idiot, okay? It's ridiculous to do some airplane thing you hate instead of doing some Rat Pack thing you love.
Besides, why isn't anyone else allowed to like Frank Sinatra?
Because they don't even really like him. They're just mindless trendoids following the herd. I make up my own mind—I'm not a superficial popularity junkie.

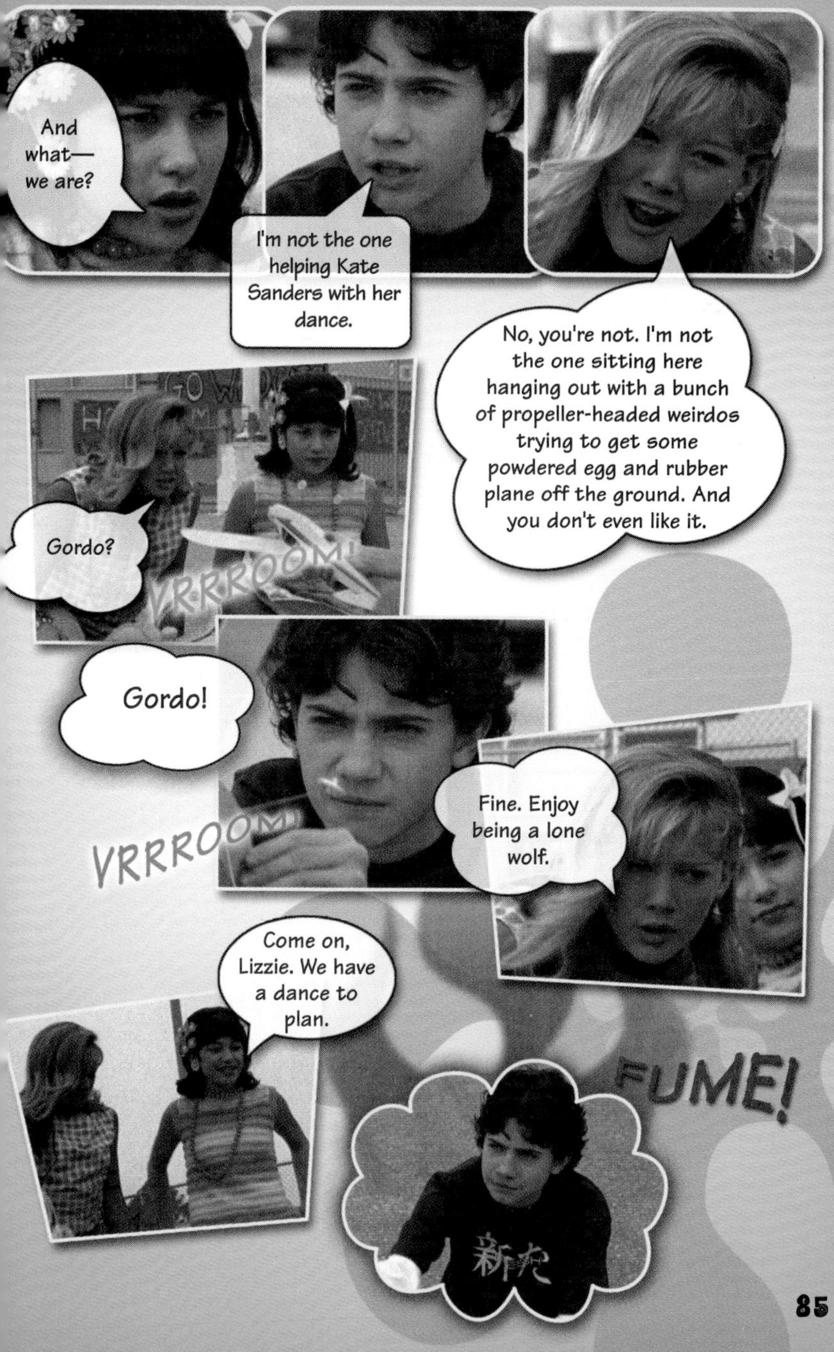
And what— we are?
I'm not the one helping Kate Sanders with her dance.
No, you're not. I'm not the one sitting here hanging out with a bunch of propeller-headed weirdos trying to get some powdered egg and rubber plane off the ground. And you don't even like it.
Gordo?
VRRROOM!
Gordo!
VRRROOM!
Fine. Enjoy being a lone wolf.
Come on, Lizzie. We have a dance to plan.
FUME!

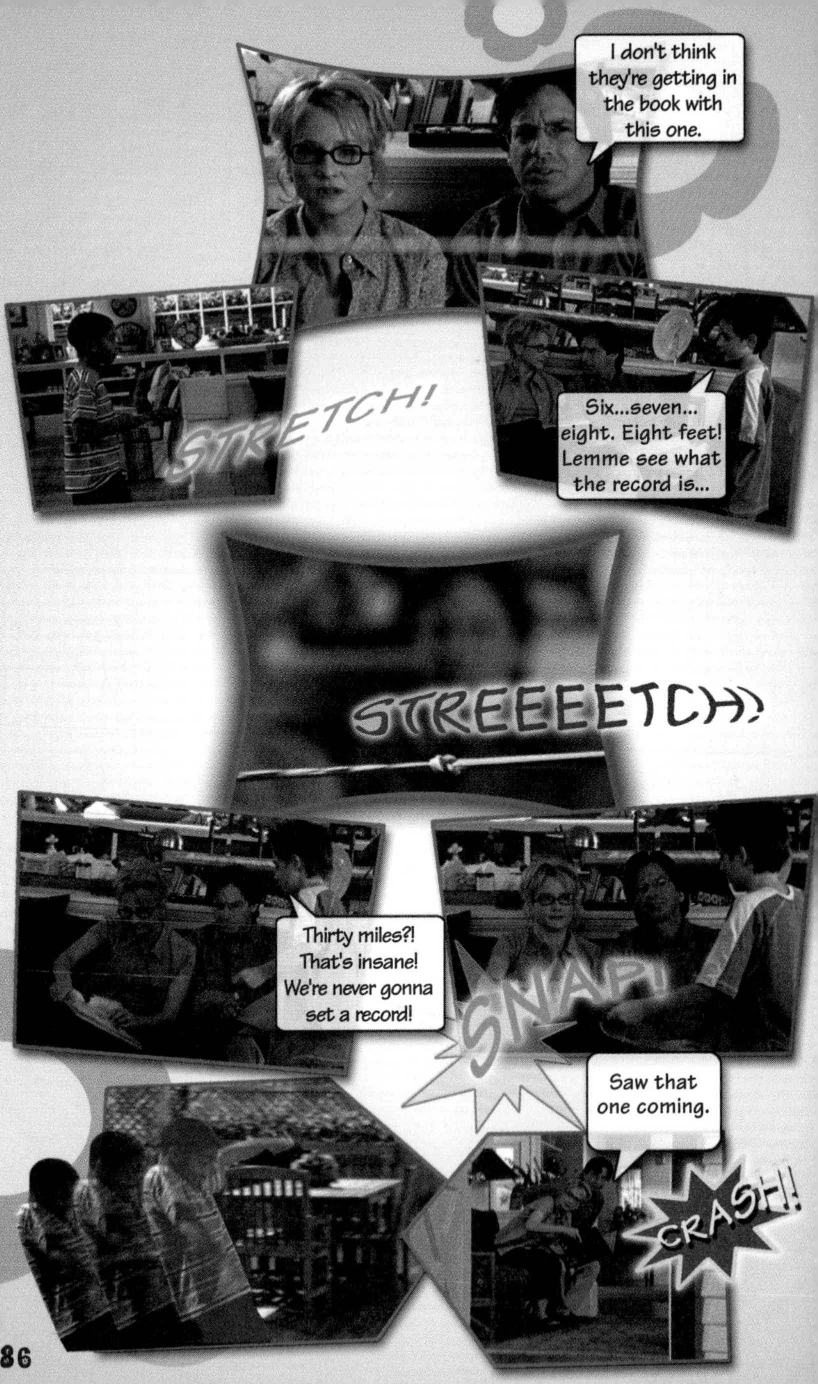
I don't think they're getting in the book with this one.
STRETCH!
Six...seven... eight. Eight feet! Lemme see what the record is...
STREEEEETCH!
Thirty miles?! That's insane! We're never gonna set a record!
SNAP!
Saw that one coming.
CRASH!

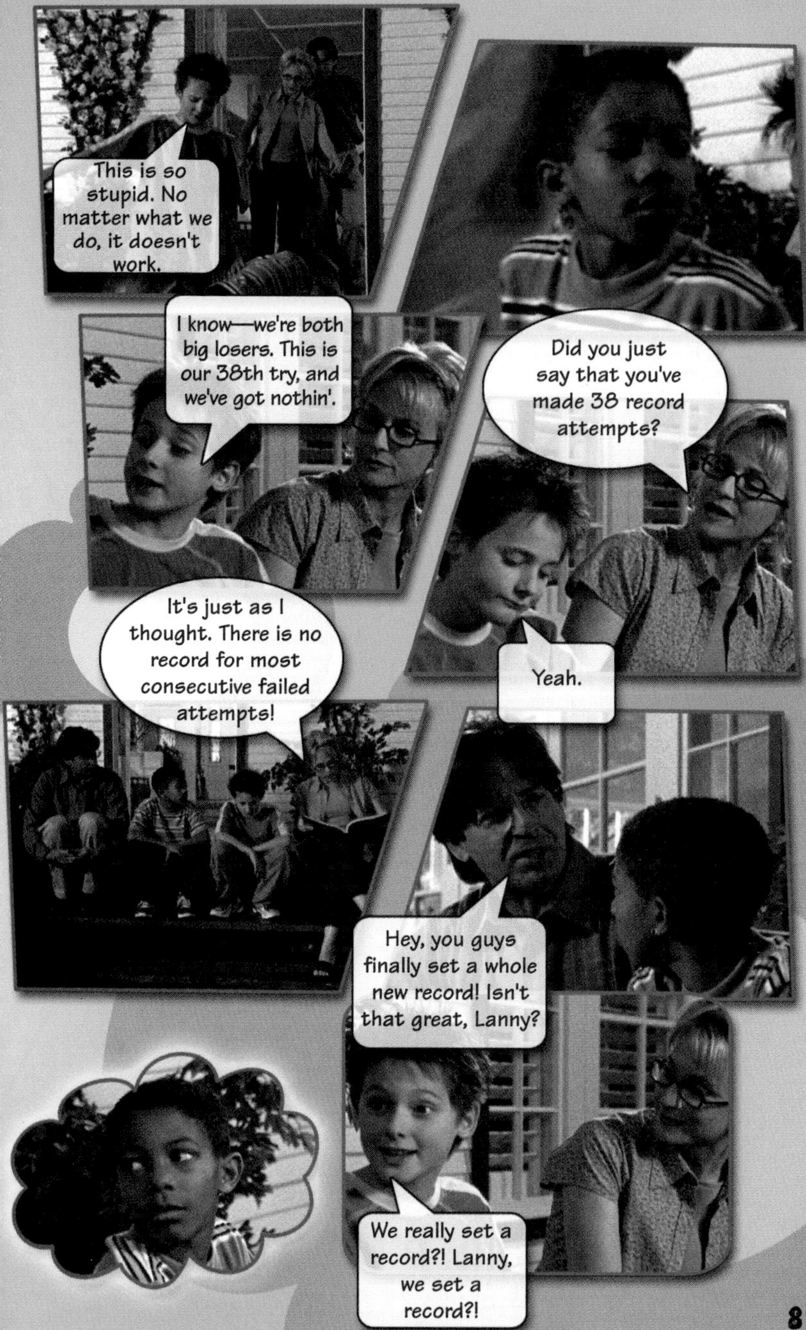
This is so stupid. No matter what we do, it doesn't work.
I know—we're both big losers. This is our 38th try, and we've got nothin'.
Did you just say that you've made 38 record attempts?
Yeah.
It's just as I thought. There is no record for most consecutive failed attempts!
Hey, you guys finally set a whole new record! Isn't that great, Lanny?
We really set a record?! Lanny, we set a record?!

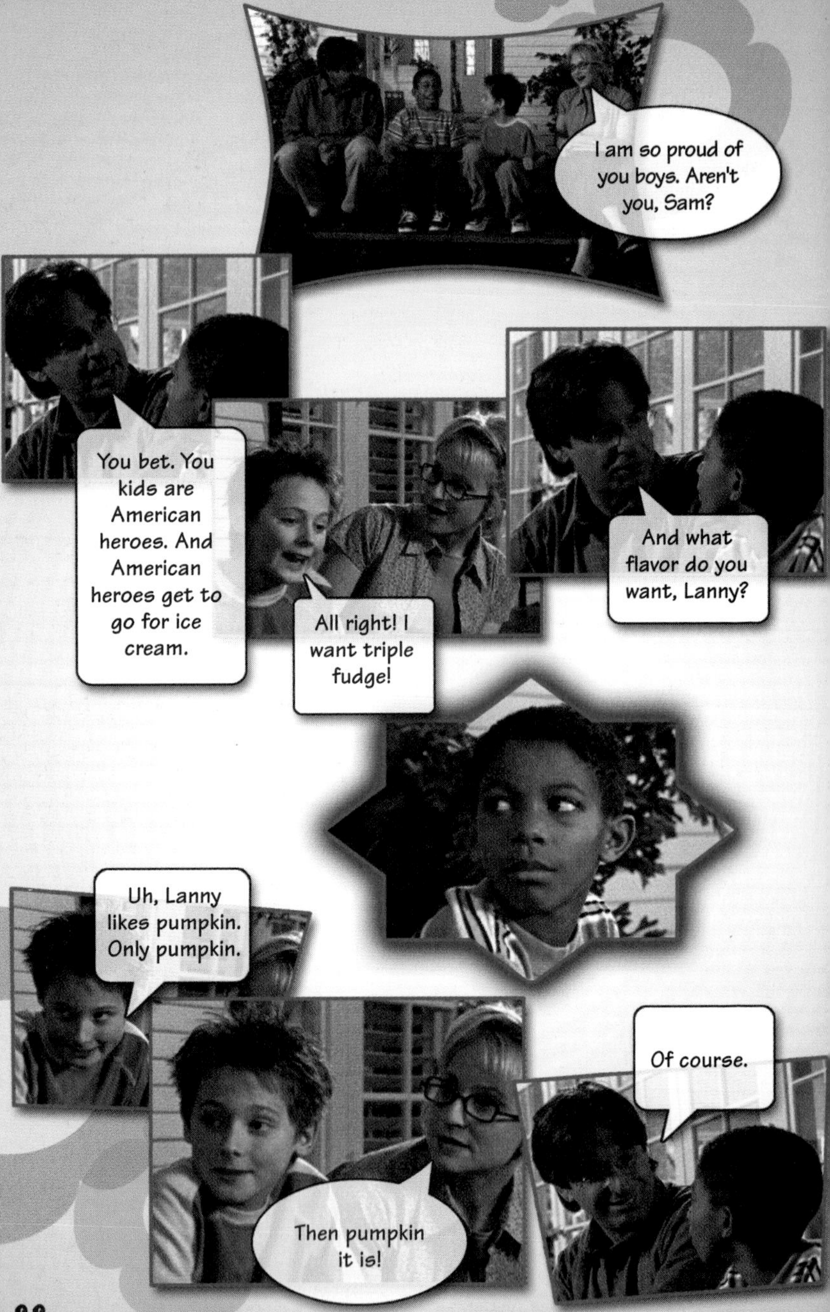
I am so proud of you boys. Aren't you, Sam?
You bet. You kids are American heroes. And American heroes get to go for ice cream.
All right! I want triple fudge!
And what flavor do you want, Lanny?
Uh, Lanny likes pumpkin. Only pumpkin.
Then pumpkin it is!
Of course.

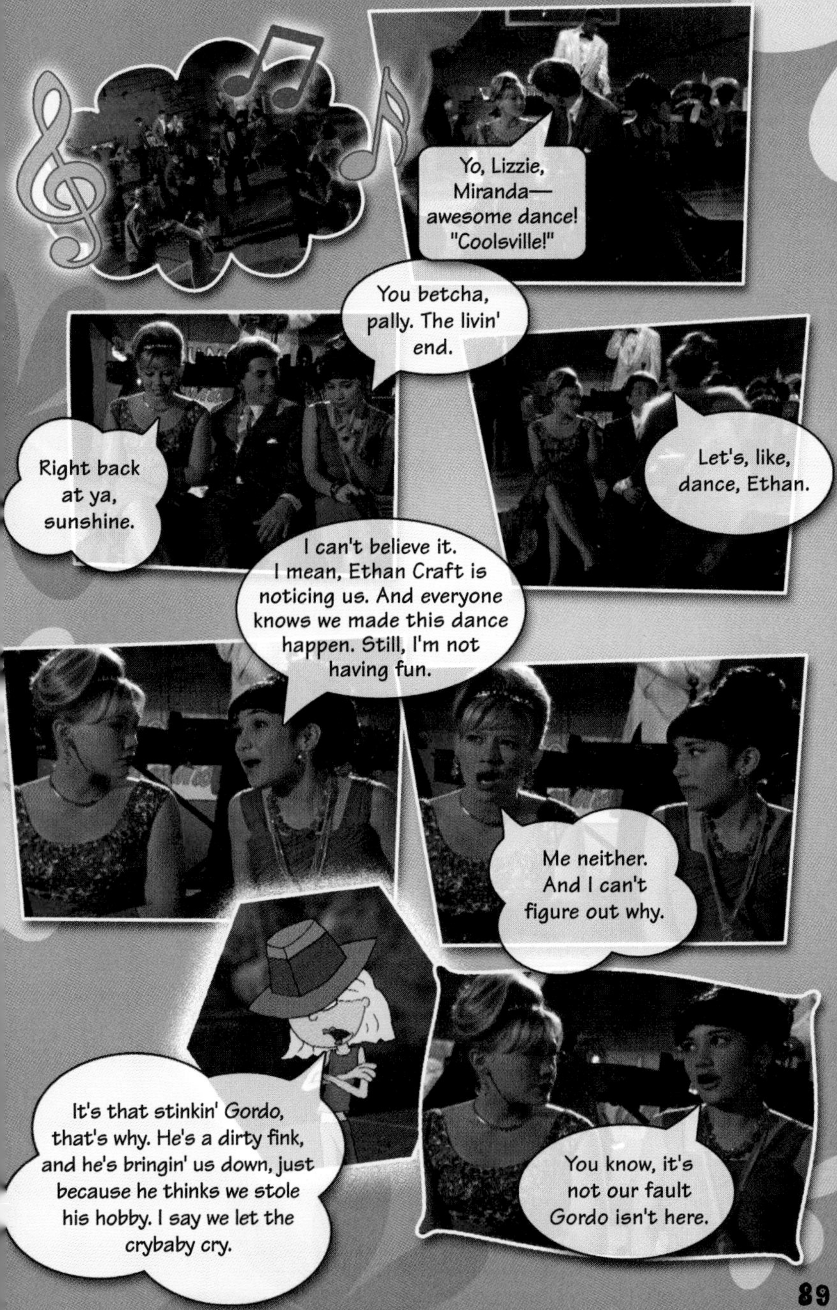
Yo, Lizzie, Miranda— awesome dance! "Coolsville!"
You betcha, pally. The livin' end.
Right back at ya, sunshine.
Let's, like, dance, Ethan.
I can't believe it. I mean, Ethan Craft is noticing us. And everyone knows we made this dance happen. Still, I'm not having fun.
Me neither. And I can't figure out why.
It's that stinkin' Gordo, that's why. He's a dirty fink, and he's bringin' us down, just because he thinks we stole his hobby. I say we let the crybaby cry.
You know, it's not our fault Gordo isn't here.

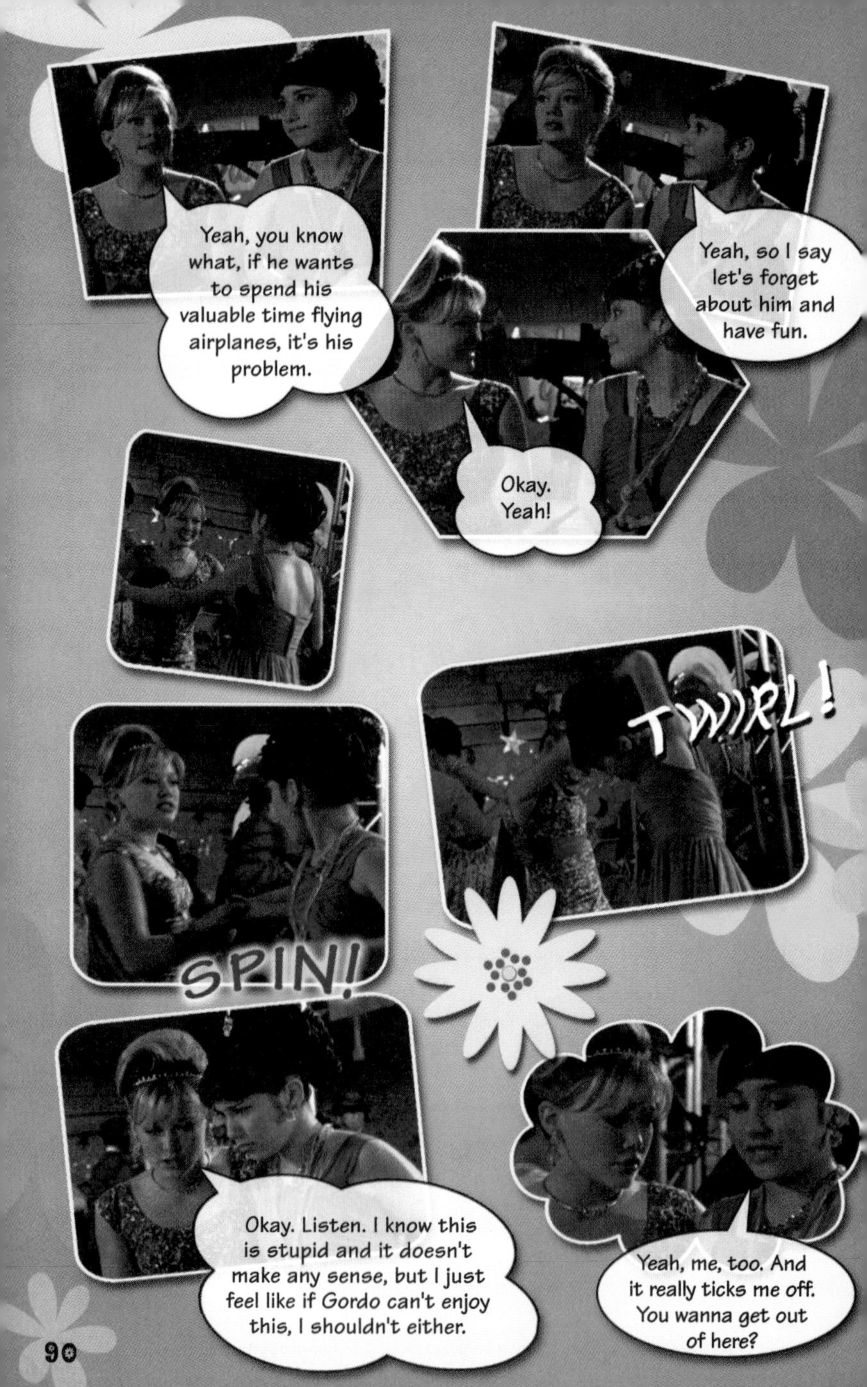
Yeah, you know what, if he wants to spend his valuable time flying airplanes, it's his problem.
Yeah, so I say let's forget about him and have fun.
Okay. Yeah!
TWIRL!
SPIN!
Okay. Listen. I know this is stupid and it doesn't make any sense, but I just feel like if Gordo can't enjoy this, I shouldn't either.
Yeah, me, too. And it really ticks me off. You wanna get out of here?

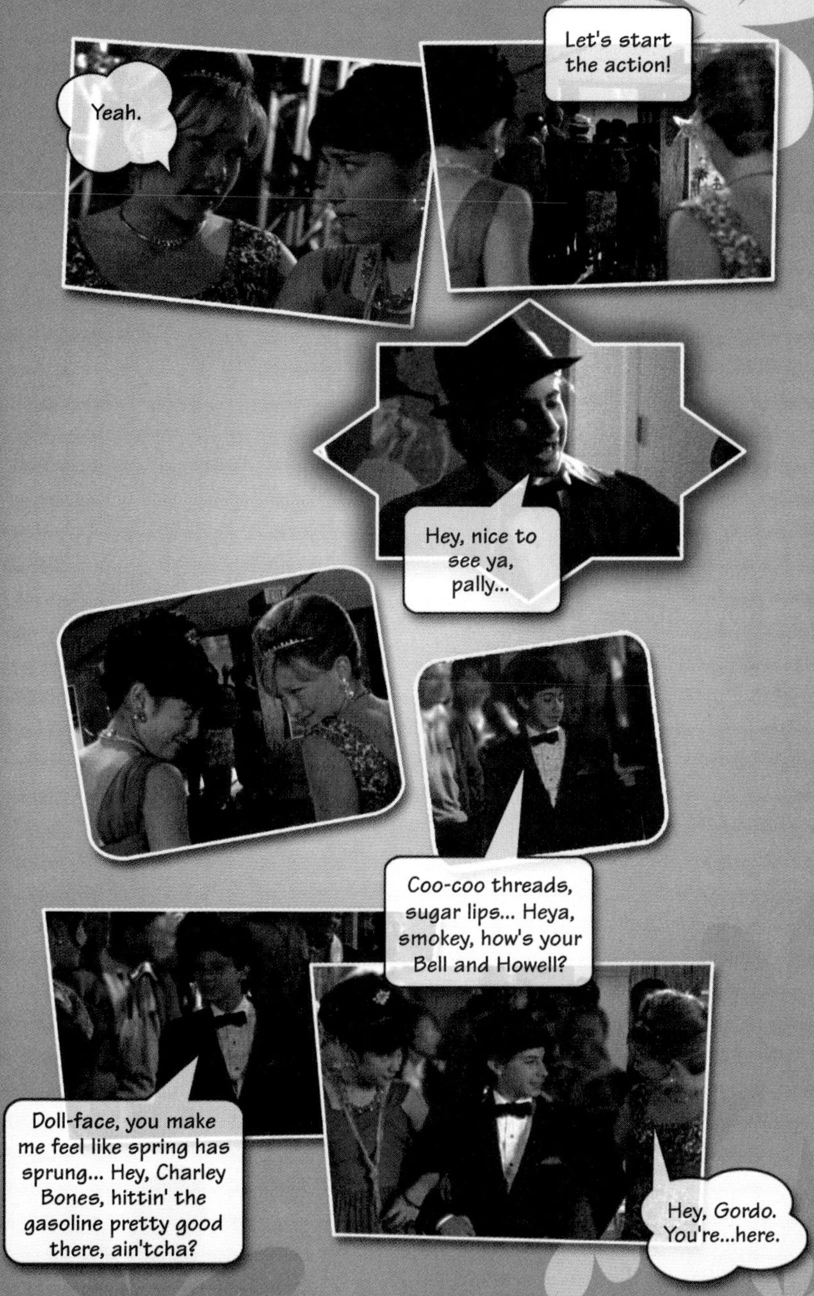
Yeah.
Let's start the action!
Hey, nice to see ya, pally...
Coo-coo threads, sugar lips... Heya, smokey, how's your Bell and Howell?
Doll-face, you make me feel like spring has sprung... Hey, Charley Bones, hittin' the gasoline pretty good there, ain'tcha?
Hey, Gordo. You're...here.

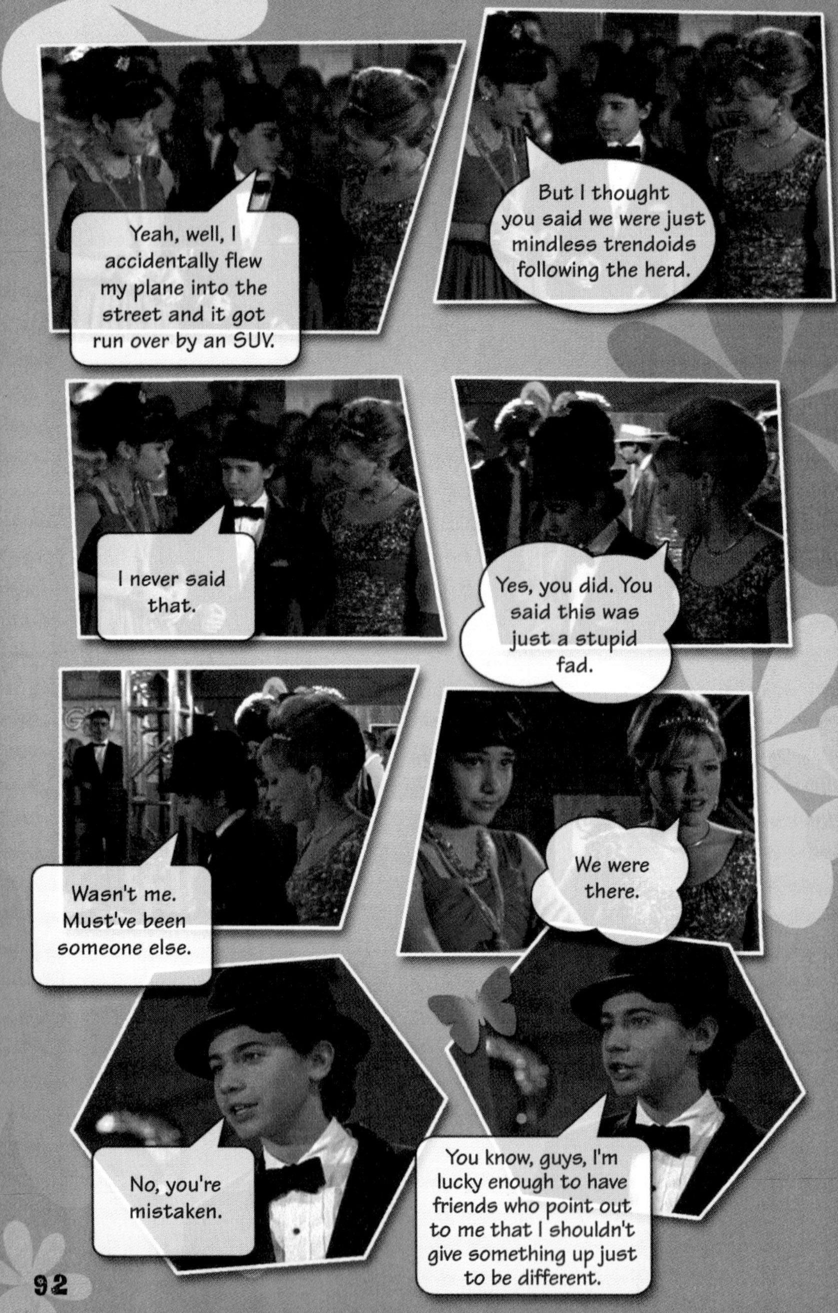
Yeah, well, I accidentally flew my plane into the street and it got run over by an SUV.
But I thought you said we were just mindless trendoids following the herd.
I never said that.
Yes, you did. You said this was just a stupid fad.
Wasn't me. Must've been someone else.
We were there.
No, you're mistaken.
You know, guys, I'm lucky enough to have friends who point out to me that I shouldn't give something up just to be different.

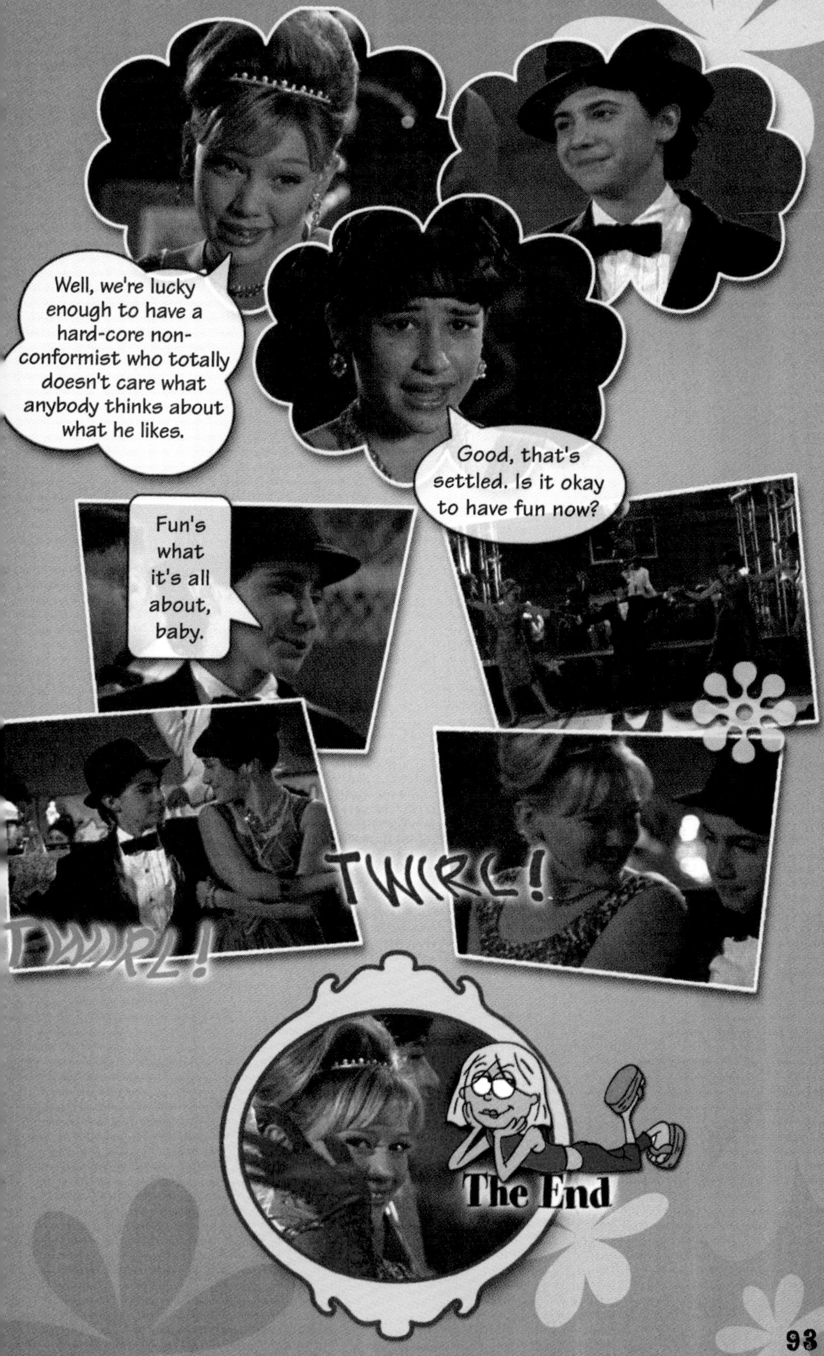

Well, we're lucky enough to have a hard-core non-conformist who totally doesn't care what anybody thinks about what he likes.
Good, that's settled. Is it okay to have fun now?
Fun's what it's all about, baby.
TWIRL!
TWIRL!
The End

Lizzie McGuire

CINE-MANGA™ VOLUME 5

COMING SOON FROM TOKYOPOP®

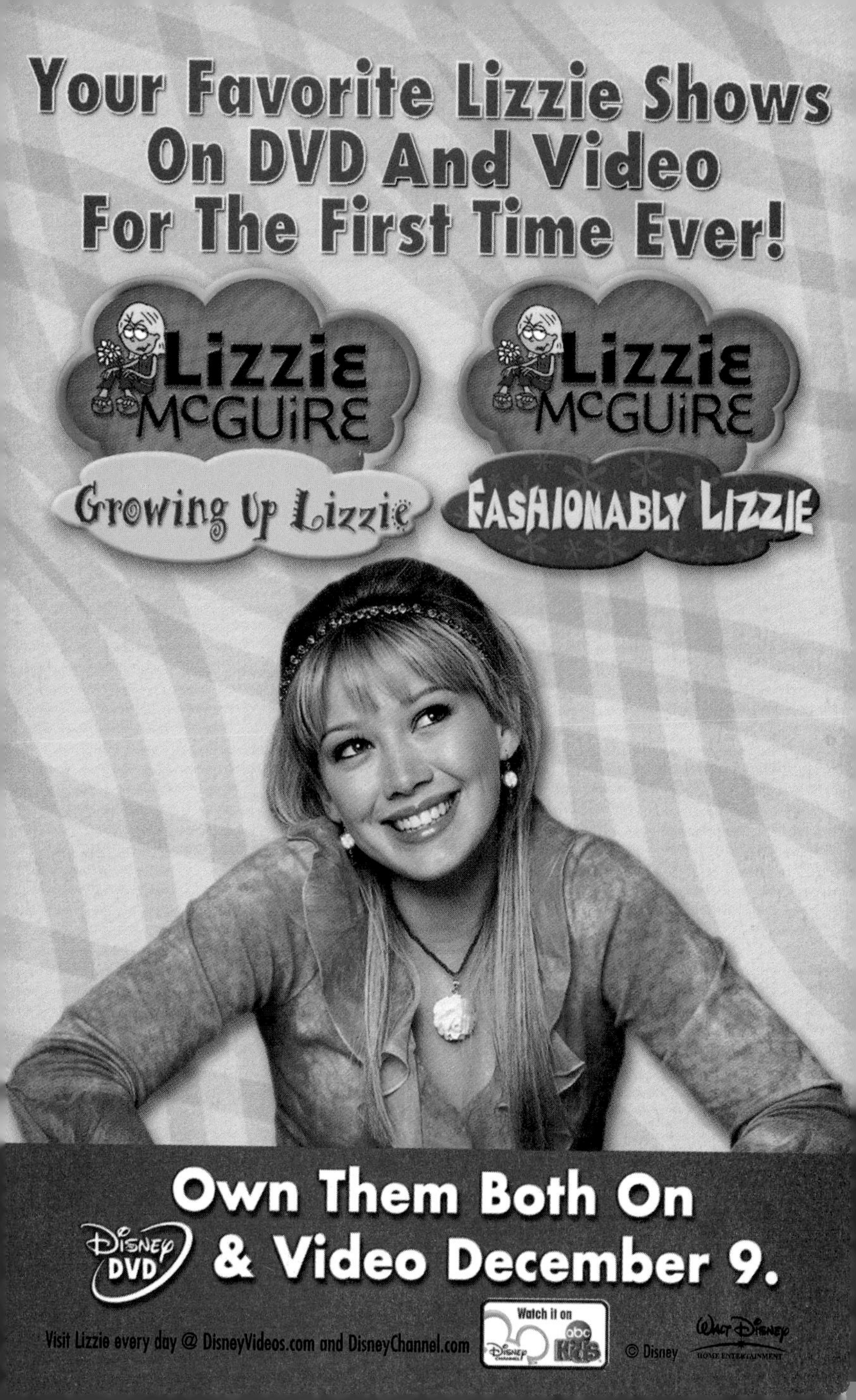

Your Favorite Lizzie Shows On DVD And Video For The First Time Ever!
Lizzie McGuire
Growing Up Lizzie
Lizzie McGuire
Fashionably Lizzie
Own Them Both On
Disney DVD & Video December 9.
Visit Lizzie every day @ DisneyVideos.com and DisneyChannel.com
Watch it on
Disney Channel
abc Kids
© Disney
Walt Disney Home Entertainment

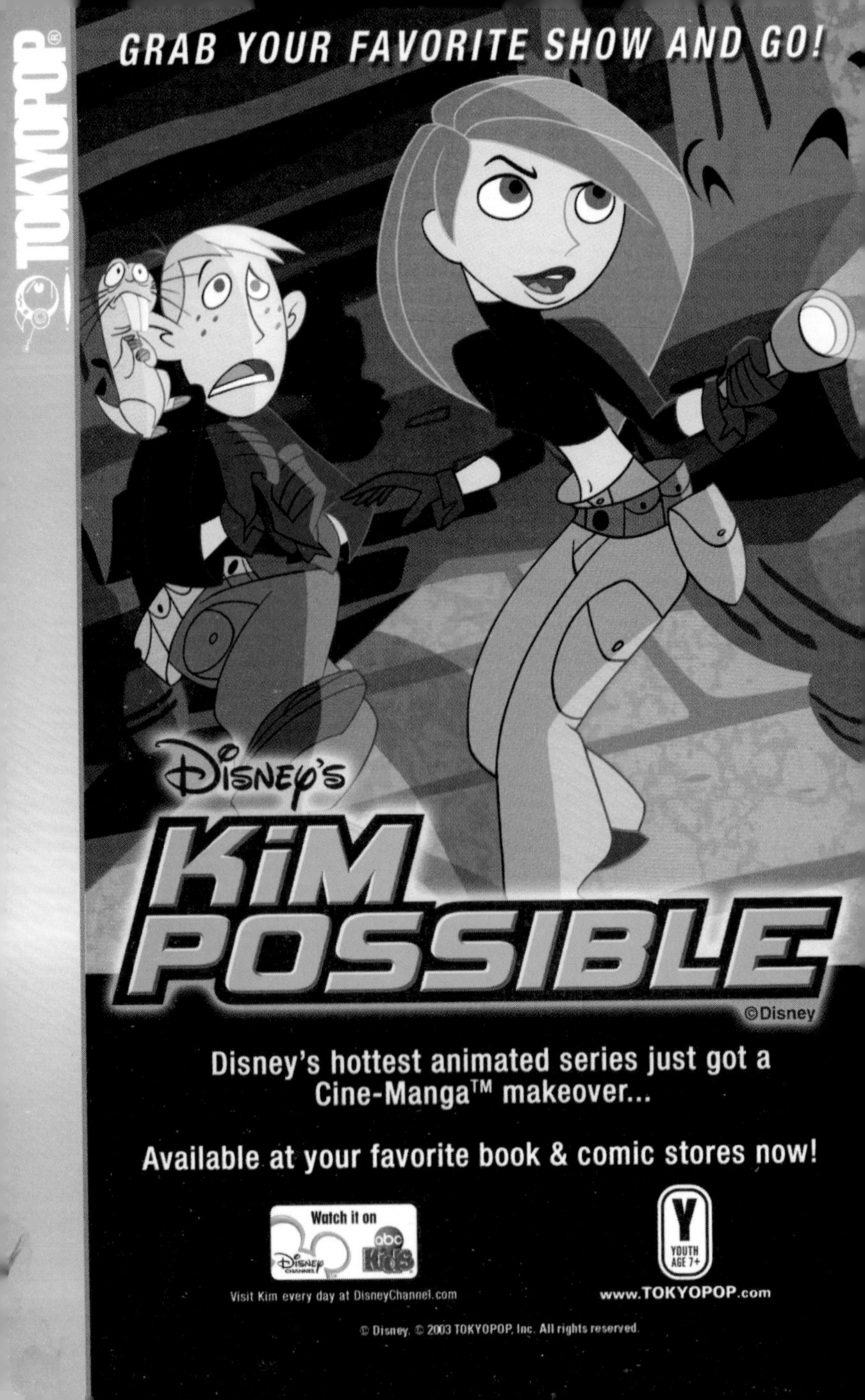
TOKYOPOP
GRAB YOUR FAVORITE SHOW AND GO!
Disney's
Kim Possible
©Disney
Disney's hottest animated series just got a Cine-Manga™ makeover...
Available at your favorite book & comic stores now!
Watch it on
Disney Channel
abc Kids
Y
YOUTH AGE 7+
Visit Kim every day at DisneyChannel.com
www.TOKYOPOP.com
© Disney. © 2003 TOKYOPOP, Inc. All rights reserved.